FUN EXPERIMENTS WITH SCIENCE AND MATHS

on Paper

Roy Richards

SIMON & SCHUSTER

LONDON • SYDNEY • NEW YORK • TOKYO • SINGAPORE • TORONTO

Contents

First published in 1990
by Simon & Schuster Young Books

Simon & Schuster Young Books
Simon & Schuster Ltd
Wolsey House, Wolsey Road
Hemel Hempstead, Herts HP2 4SS

Text © 1990 Roy Richards
Designed by David West
Children's Book Design
Illustrated by Alex Pang
Illustrations © 1990 Simon & Schuster

Printed and bound in Belgium
by Proost International Book Production

British Library Cataloguing in Publication
Data
Richards, Roy
    101 science tricks.
    On paper.
    1. Primary schools. Curriculum subjects.
    Science. Activities using paper
    I. Title
    372.35

ISBN 0–7500–0284–0

PLAYING CARDS

Try building things with cards.

1 Build a house of cards. Lean two cards together to make a tent shape. Make another tent shape alongside and then put a card across the top. Continue in this way to build the bottom layer. Build a second layer on top of the first. Can you use all the cards in the pack without it toppling over?

2 How tall a tower can you build with six cards as your base? How tall a tower can you build on just three cards as a base?

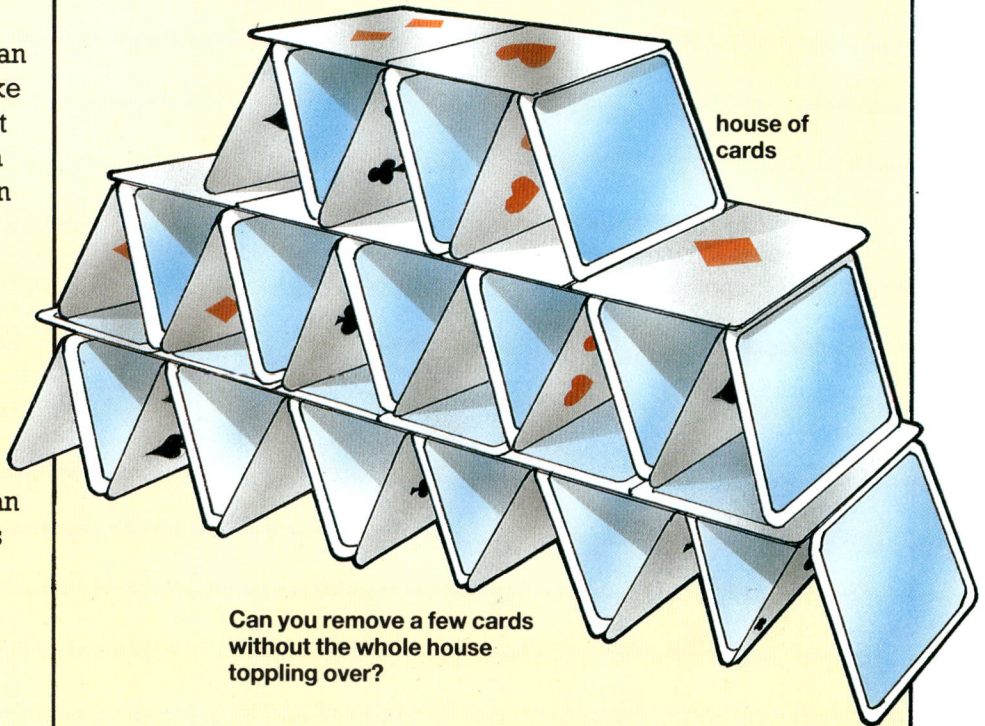

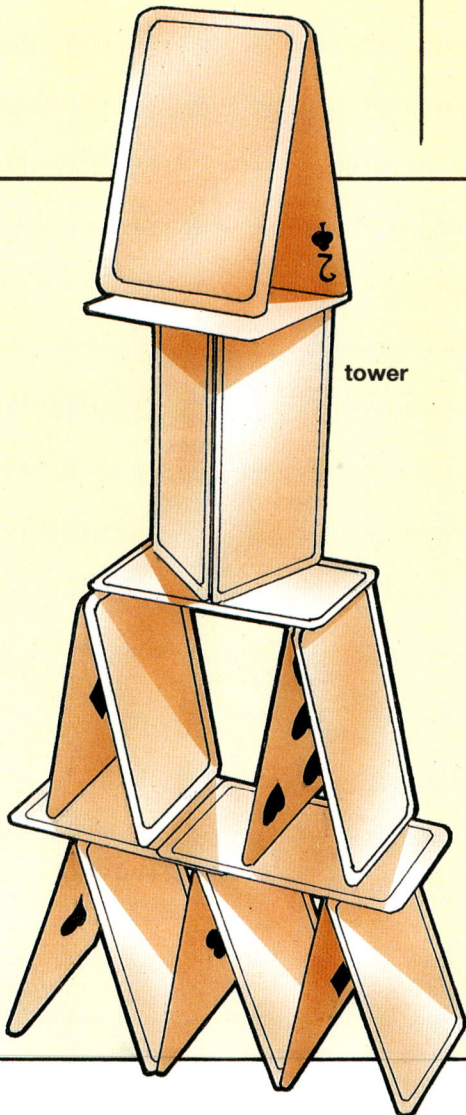

house of cards

Can you remove a few cards without the whole house toppling over?

tower

tower

6 cards as a base

3 cards as a base

BALANCING BILL

1 Trace the figure of Balancing Bill onto thick card. Cut it out.

2 You will now need to balance him. Use a tightrope made from thin string tied between two plastic bottles filled with sand or soil. Attach Bill to the tightrope. He may balance, he may fall off. If he falls off you need to make some counterbalances.

1 draw round outline of Bill cut shape out from thick card

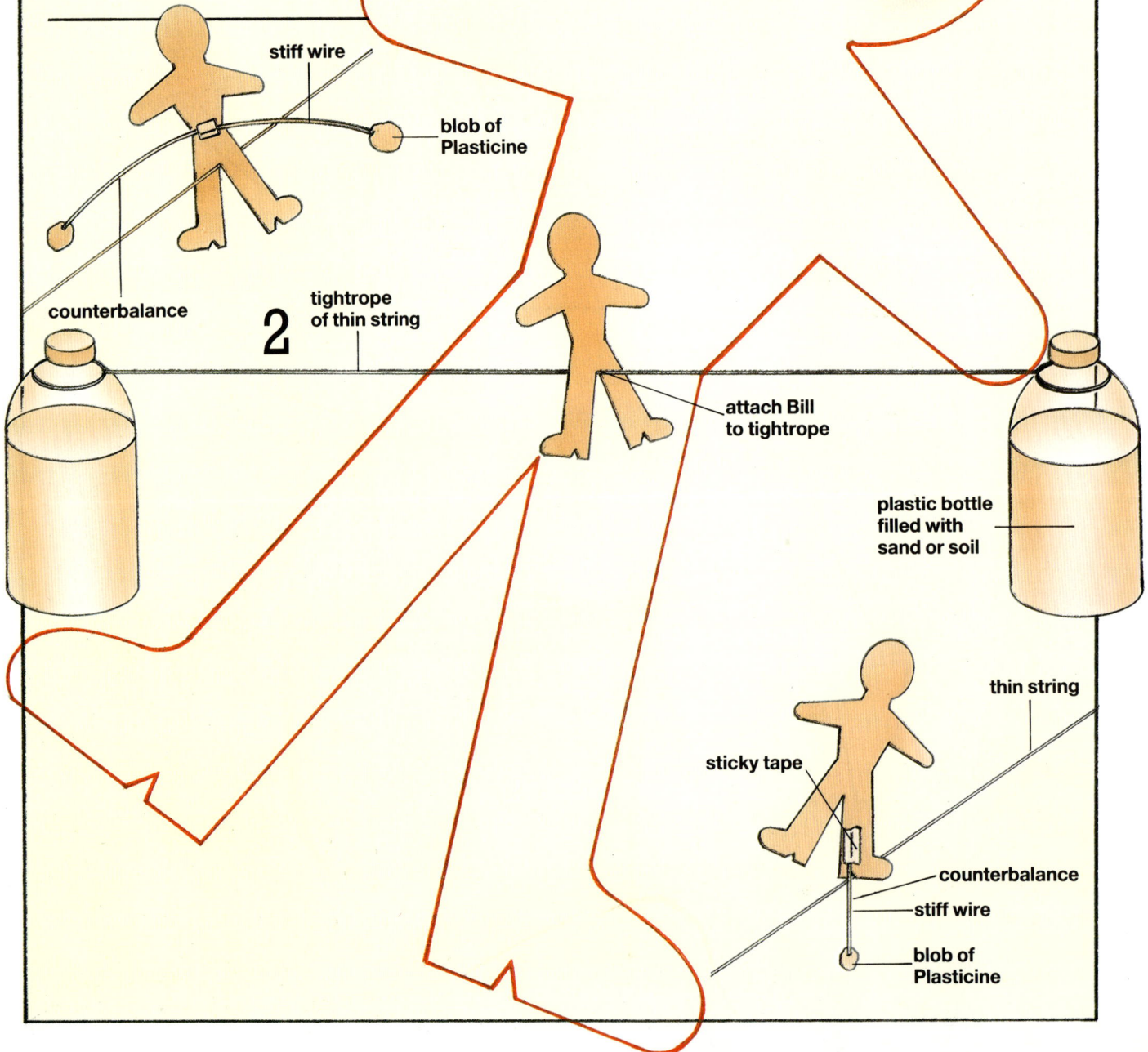

stiff wire

blob of Plasticine

counterbalance

2 tightrope of thin string

attach Bill to tightrope

plastic bottle filled with sand or soil

thin string

sticky tape

counterbalance

stiff wire

blob of Plasticine

BALANCING JILL

1 Make this figure from a cork and matchsticks. Copy Jill's face onto a circle of thick card and tape it to a matchstick. Push the matchstick into the cork body. Insert other matchsticks as shown.

2 Cut a notch in one leg. Insert forks and try balancing Jill.

3 Blow gently to make her move.

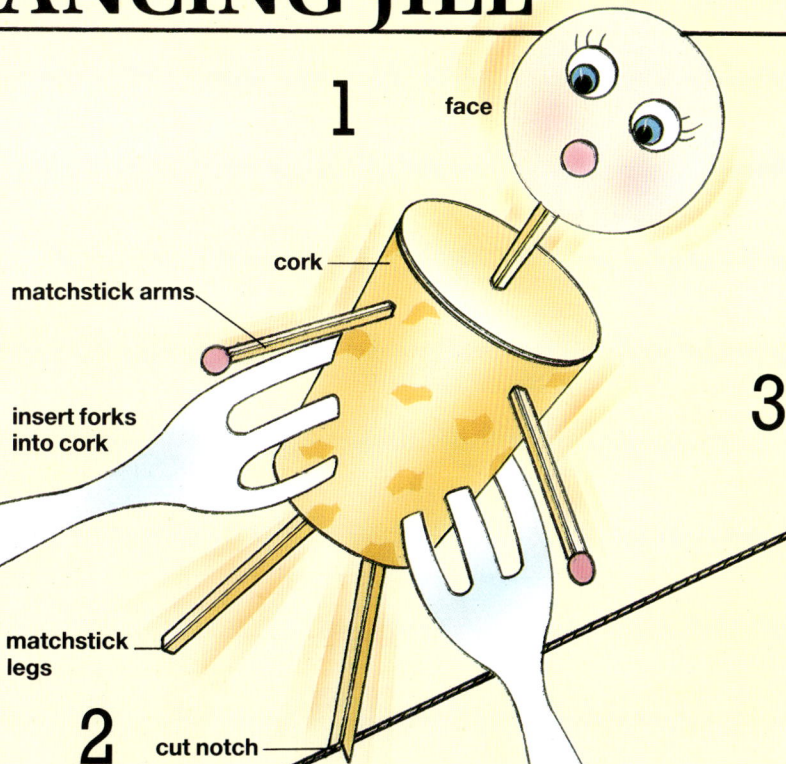

1

face

cork

matchstick arms

insert forks into cork

matchstick legs

3

2 cut notch

circle of thick card

sticky tape

matchstick

FISHERMAN PHIL

Fisherman Phil, like Jill, is made from cork, matchsticks and card. His fishing line is made from a piece of stiff wire. To make his fish trace the large fish shape shown below.

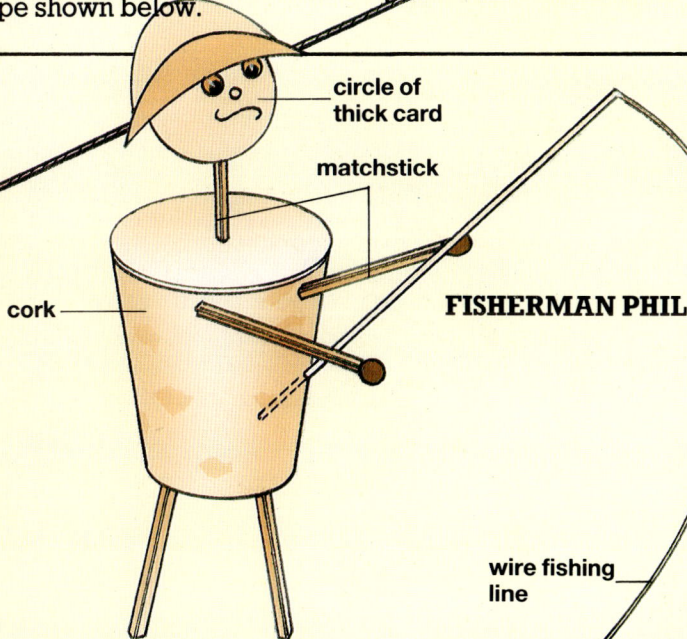

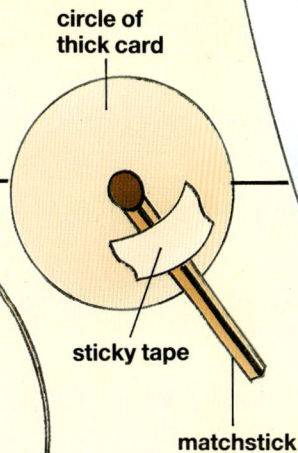

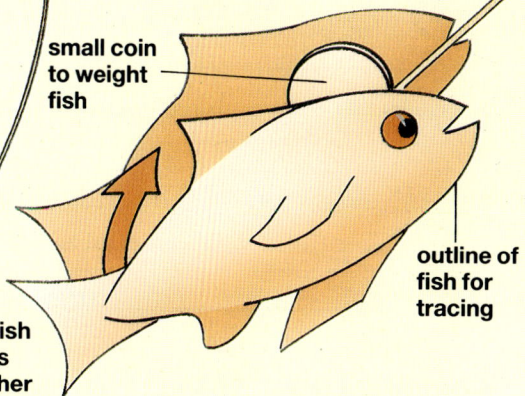

circle of thick card

matchstick

cork

FISHERMAN PHIL

small coin to weight fish

wire fishing line

outline of fish for tracing

Try balancing him on the edge of a table.

glue fish halves together

Lie the end of the wire fishing line alongside the coin and glue the two halves of the fish together.

FIERCESOME FRED

1 Trace and cut the large face of Fred from thick card and colour it in.

2 Balance him on the end of a ruler or the edge of a table as shown below. Use a paper-clip to help you get a good balance. You need to move it about to find the best balancing point.

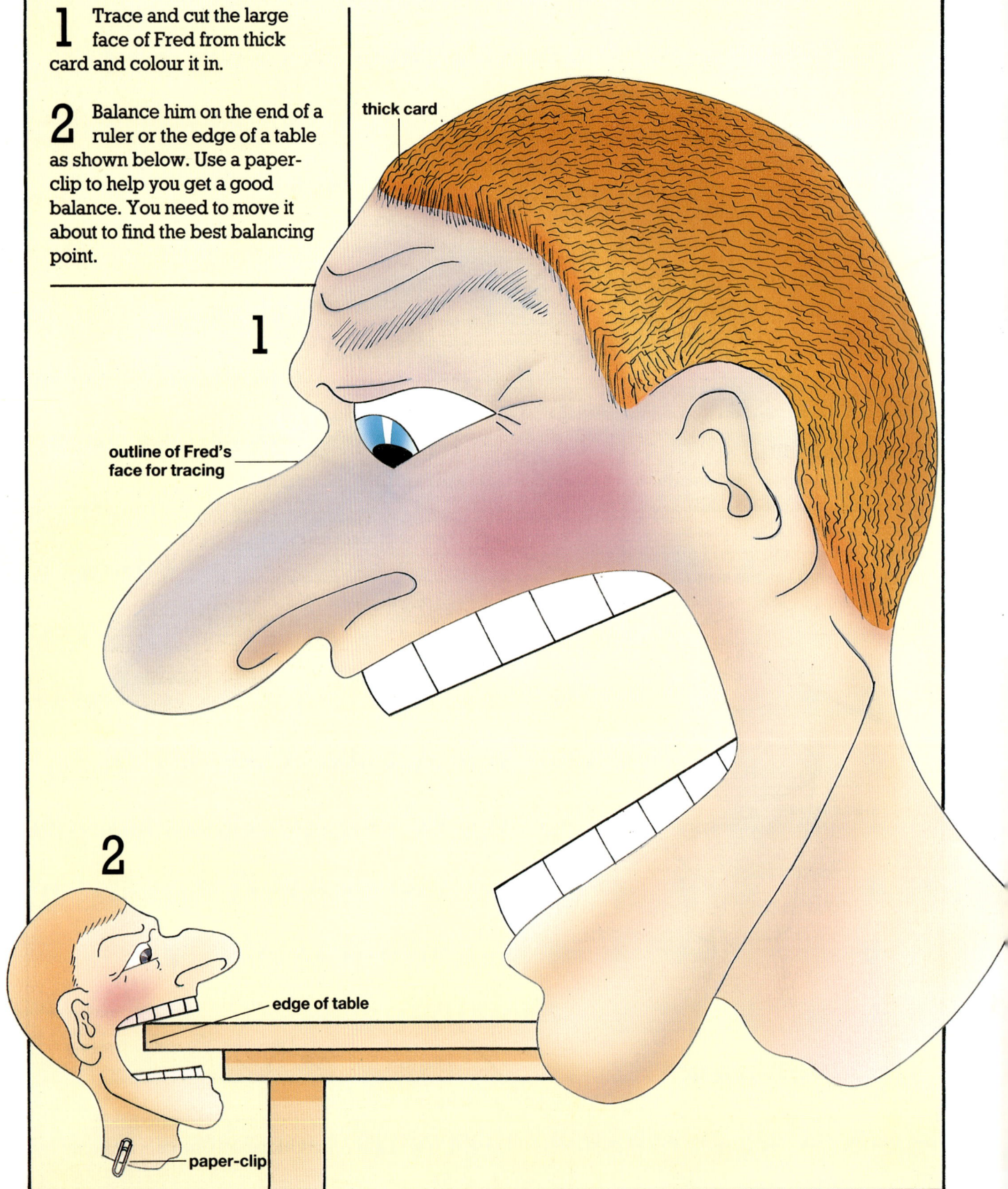

thick card

1

outline of Fred's face for tracing

2

edge of table

paper-clip

BALANCING BOYS

This toy is made from card, balsa wood, wire and Plasticine.

1 Shape a piece of balsa wood, as shown.

2 Draw and cut the see-saw and the two boys from card. Colour them in. Glue the boys to the see-saw and the see-saw to the balsa wood pivot.

3 Shape a piece of Plasticine into a ball. Attach it to the stiff wire to make a counterweight as shown. This will help you get a good balance.

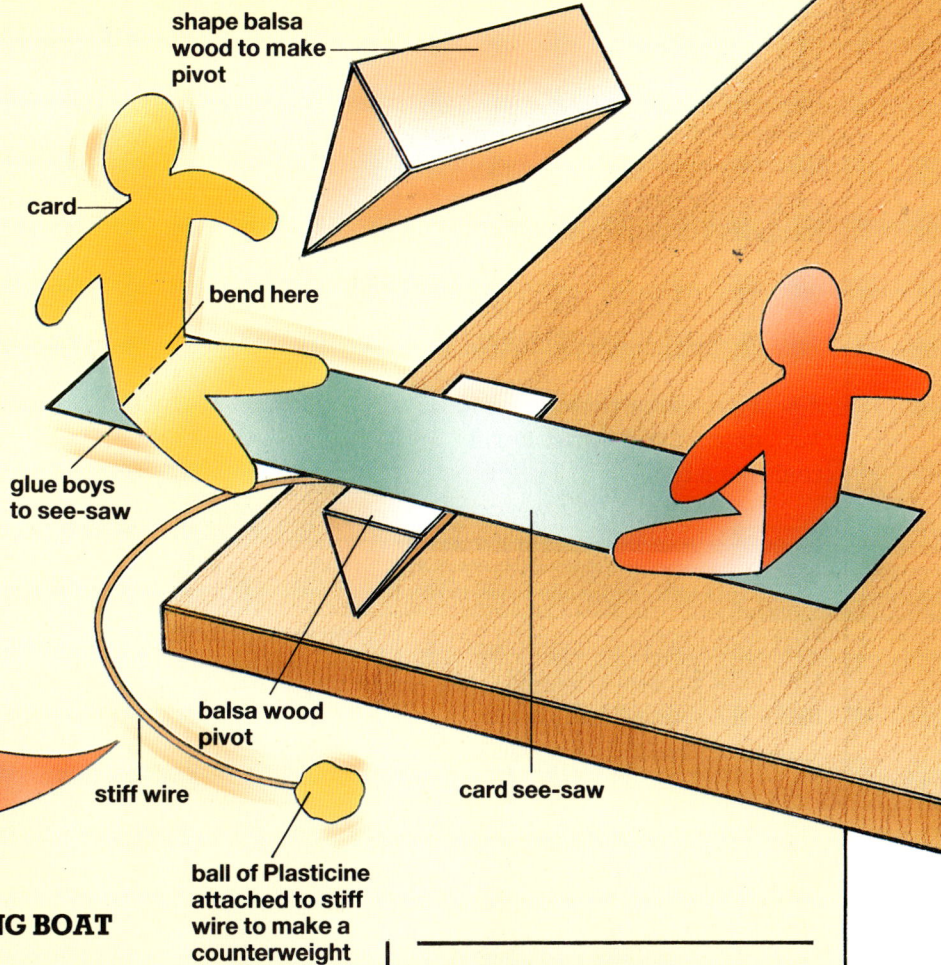

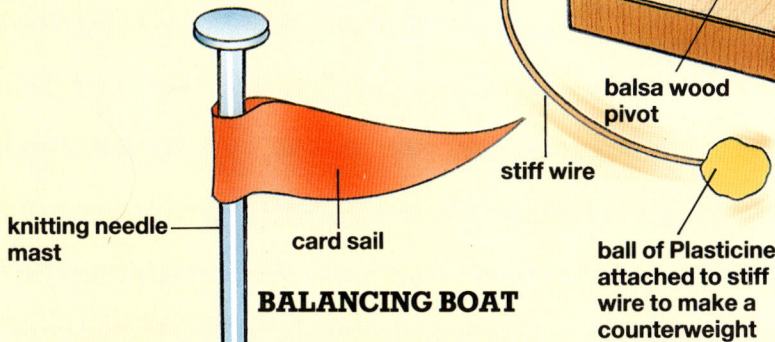

shape balsa wood to make pivot

card

bend here

glue boys to see-saw

balsa wood pivot

stiff wire

card see-saw

ball of Plasticine attached to stiff wire to make a counterweight

knitting needle mast

card sail

BALANCING BOAT

Plasticine

tennis ball

counterweight wire thrust through tennis ball and into Plasticine

stiff wire

ball of Plasticine

BALANCING BOAT

1 Cut an old tennis ball in half.

2 Make a counterweight from Plasticine and wire as before.

3 Take another piece of Plasticine and stick it inside the tennis ball. Thrust the wire of the counterweight through the tennis ball and into your Plasticine.

4 Add a knitting needle mast and a card sail if you want.

You can probably make this balance without its counterweight if you are clever!

BULL ROARER

1 Cut a piece of heavy cardboard about 200 millimetres long by 50 millimetres wide. Round off the corners. Punch a hole at one end and thread a metre of string through. Tie securely.

2 Twist the bull roarer so that you give it a slight bend.

3 Find a clear space. Swing it around your head. It will roar like a bull.

Decorate your bull roarer if you want.

You could have a competition with your friends to see who can make the loudest bull roarer.

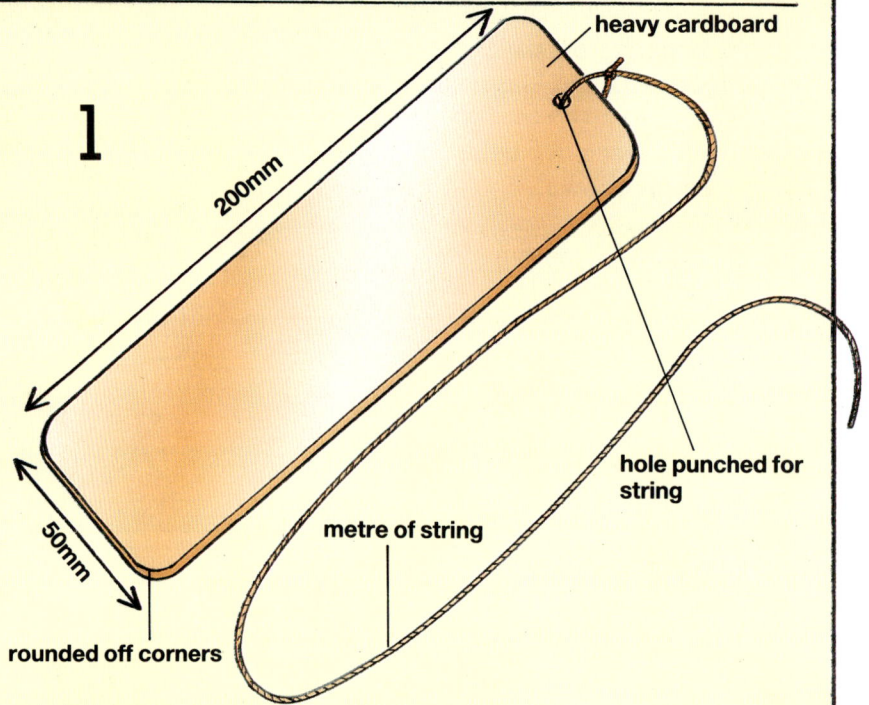

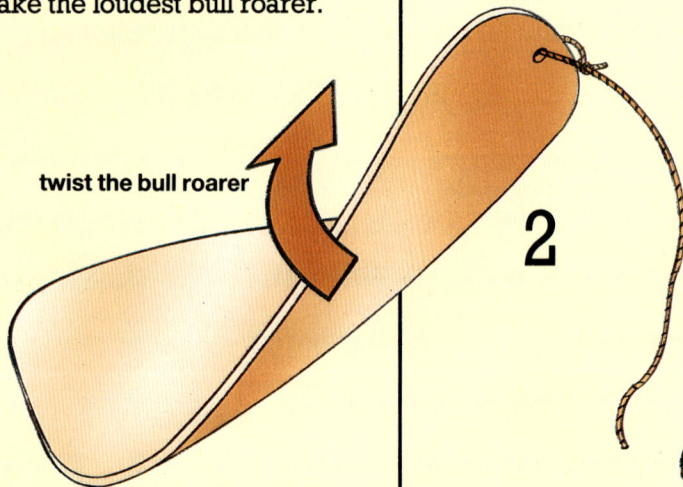

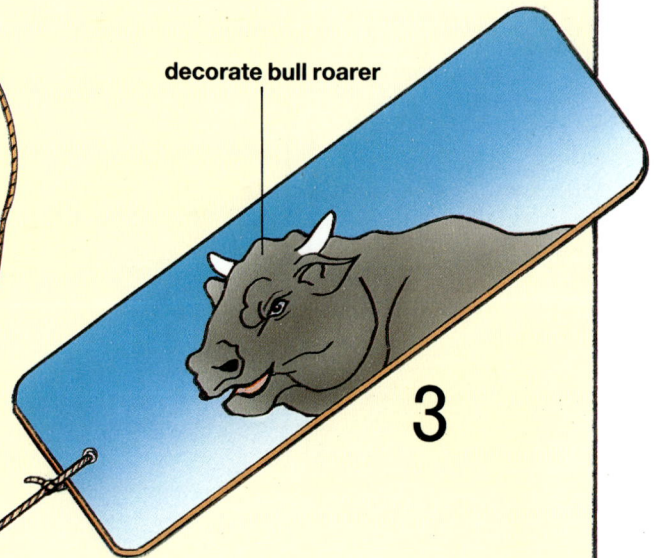

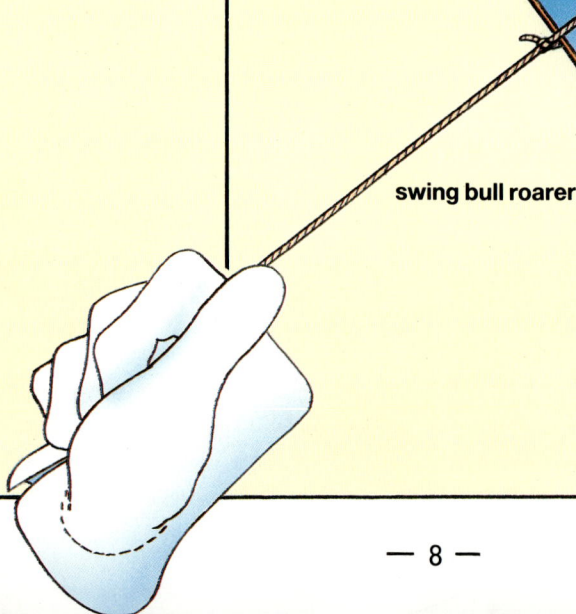

1

200mm

50mm

heavy cardboard

hole punched for string

metre of string

rounded off corners

twist the bull roarer

2

decorate bull roarer

3

swing bull roarer

BUZZ SAW

1 Trace the pattern below onto stiff card. Colour it in and cut it out.

2 Punch two holes through the card. Use the point of a a pair of compasses.

3 Thread a metre of thin string through the holes. Tie the ends.

4 Loop the ends of the string over your fingers. Pull the string outwards and then relax. Keep repeating this. The buzz saw will spin. Hold the revolving buzz saw to a sheet of paper sticking out from a table. As the teeth of the buzz saw hit the paper you will hear a buzzing noise.

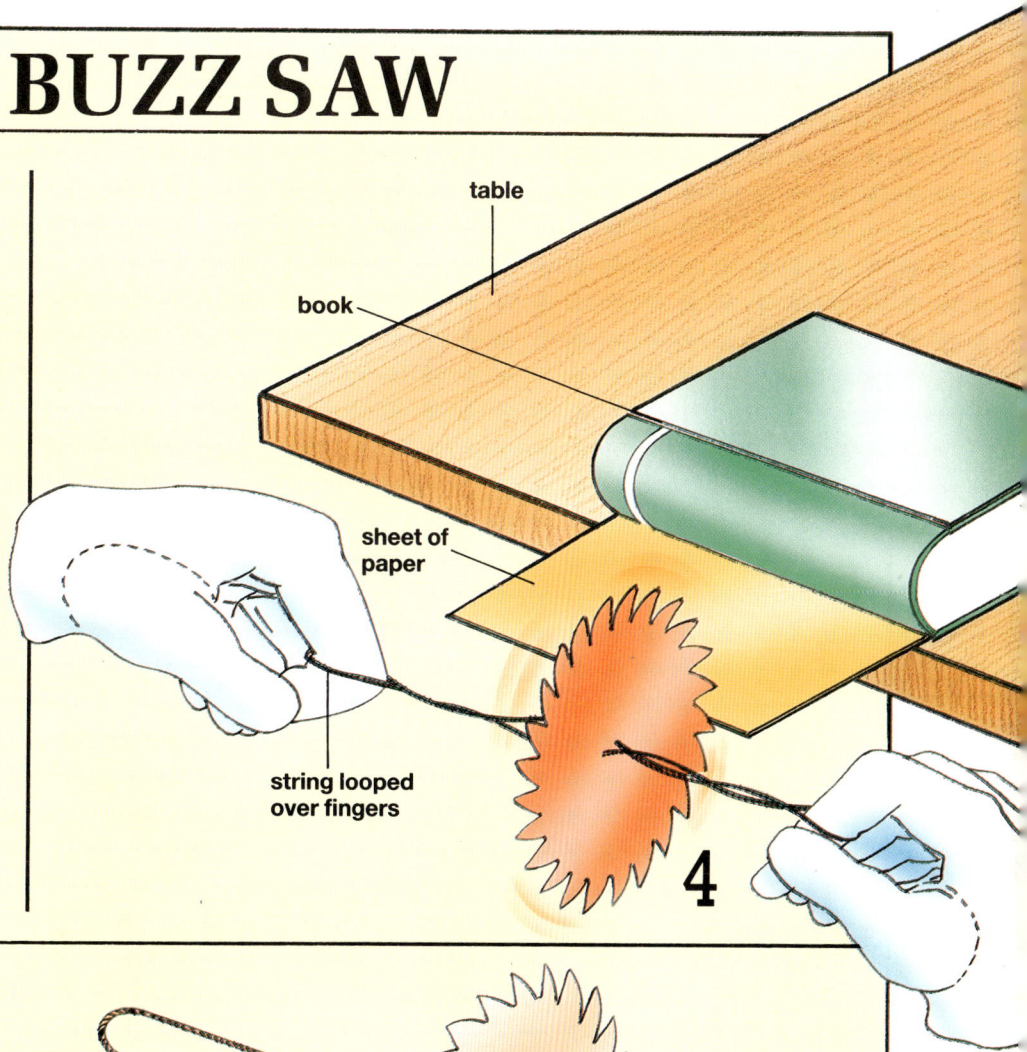

table

book

sheet of paper

string looped over fingers

4

2

punch 2 holes

3

metre of thin string

string threaded through holes

buzz saw teeth

1 pattern for tracing

cut pattern out from stiff card

POCKET SUNDIAL

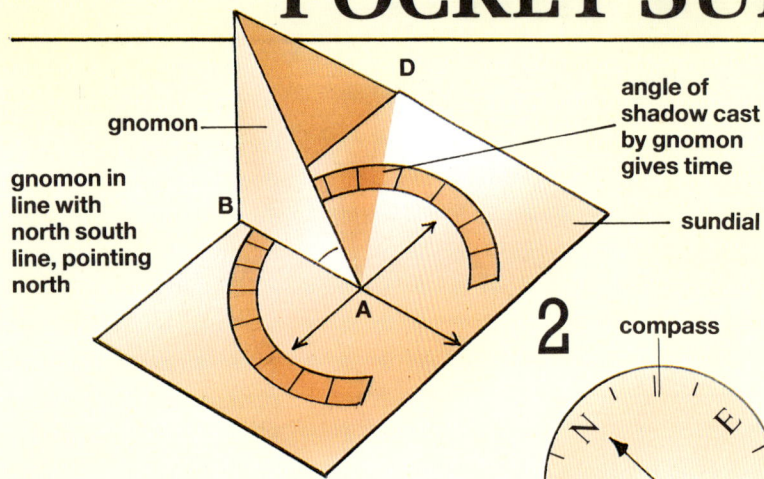

gnomon

angle of shadow cast by gnomon gives time

gnomon in line with north south line, pointing north

sundial

C
D
B
A

2

compass

N
E
W
S

The picture on the left shows a typical sundial. The raised central portion is called the gnomon. The angle of the gnomon to the horizontal varies with the angle of latitude of where you live. For example in London it is 51.5°, in New York it is 41°. You need to look up the latitude of where you live in an atlas, and make your gnomon to the angle of that latitude.

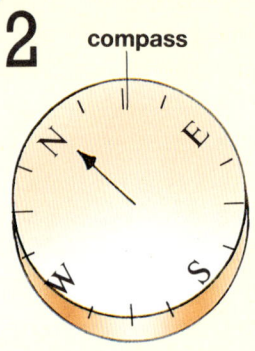

1 Trace the pattern at the bottom of the page onto stiff card. Cut it out. Cut along line A B. Score along line B C. Bend along line B C. Score along line B. D. Bend along B. D. Stand triangle A B C up as shown left so that it forms a gnomon.

2 Set the sundial with the gnomon in line with the north south line, and pointing north. On sunny days the shadow cast by the gnomon will give good time. Put the folded sundial in a small envelope. Keep it handy!

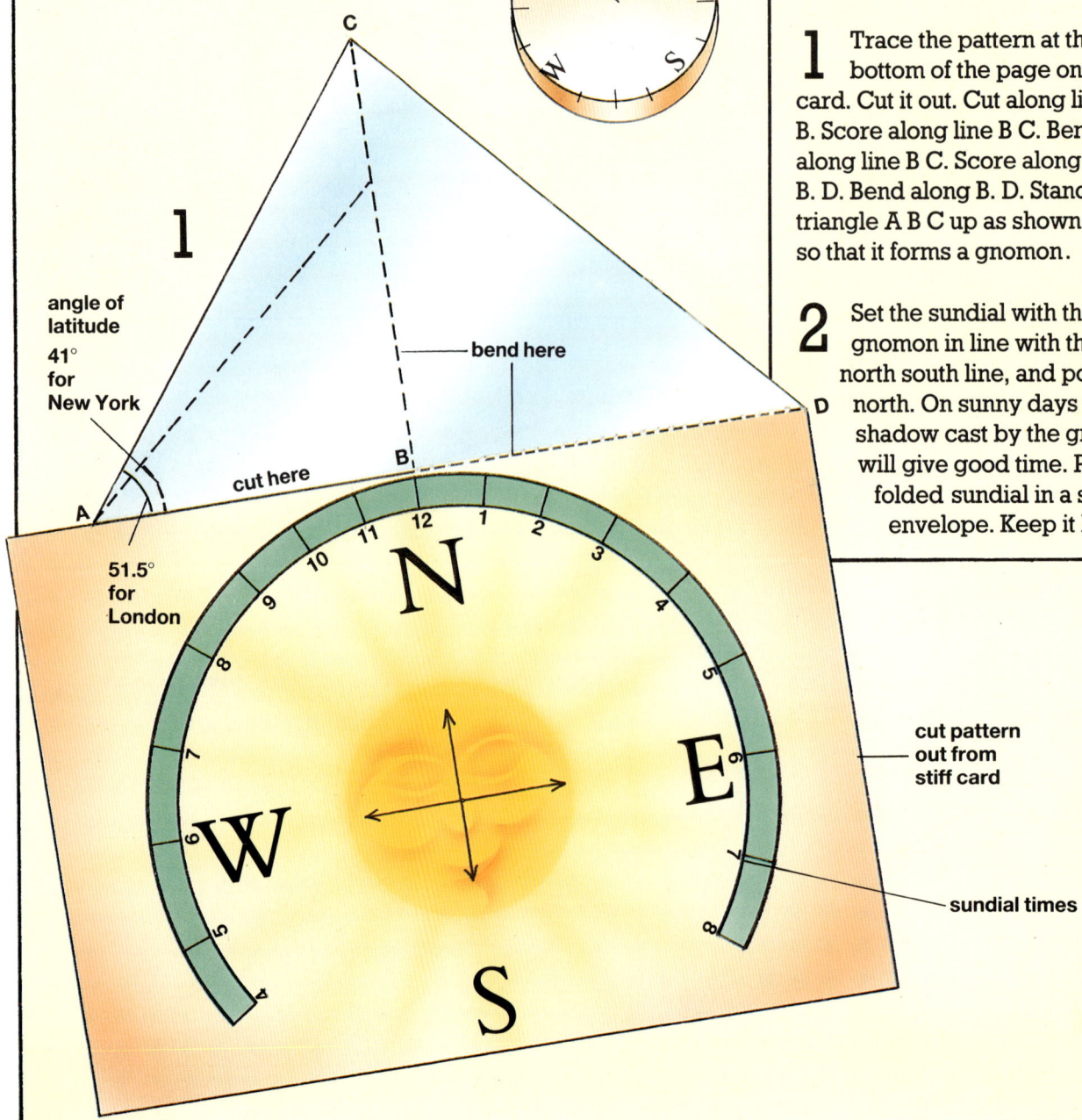

1

C

angle of latitude 41° for New York

bend here

D

cut here

B

51.5° for London

A

cut pattern out from stiff card

sundial times

10 11 12 1 2 3 4 5 6 7 8 9

N

E

W

S

STAR CLOCK

1 Cut a 150 millimetre disc from card and draw a 100 millimetre circle on it. Mark out 30 degree sectors with a protractor on the 100 millimetre circle. Draw in the Plough, Cassiopeia and the Pole Star as shown.

2 Cut a 200 millimetre disc from card and draw a 150 millimetre circle on it. Mark out a 24 hour clock on this large disc.

3 Fix the small disc to the large disc with a paper fastener. At night match the star circle with the Plough constellation in the sky. Note the time and arrange the clock circle against the pointers of the Plough.

An hour later check the position of the Plough. Match the star circle to the Plough again. You will find it rotates to your 24 hour clock.

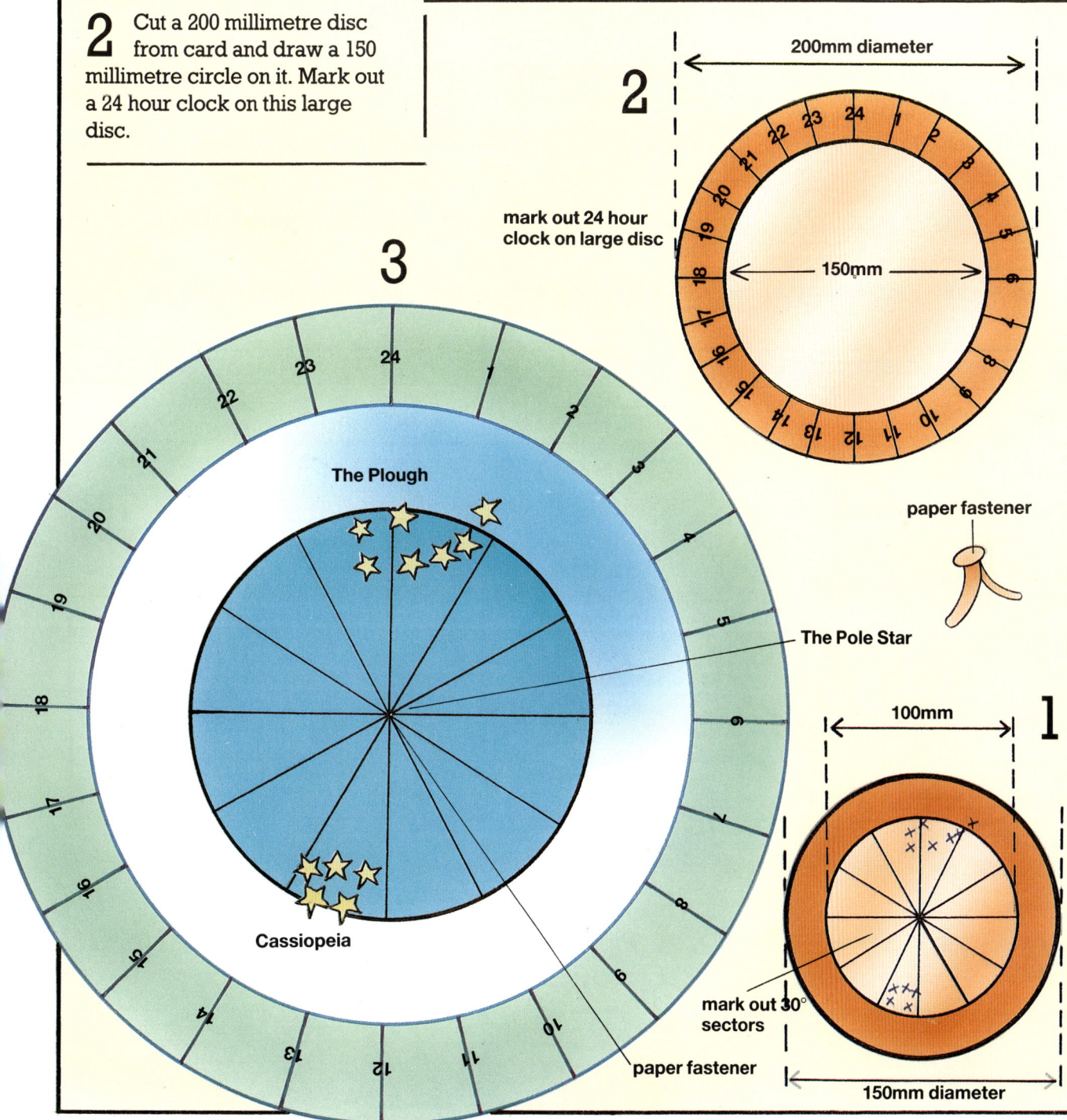

2

200mm diameter

mark out 24 hour clock on large disc

150mm

3

The Plough

The Pole Star

paper fastener

Cassiopeia

1

100mm

mark out 30° sectors

paper fastener

150mm diameter

REVOLVING SNAKE

1 Trace this snake onto thin card or paper.

2 Cut it out. Cut along the line of the snake.

3 Make a pin prick through the snake's tail.

Thread cotton through the hole. Tie two or three knots.

4 Hold the snake above the table lamp. The heat current rising from the lamp will cause the snake to revolve.

A snake hung above a radiator will turn all day – if the radiator is left on.

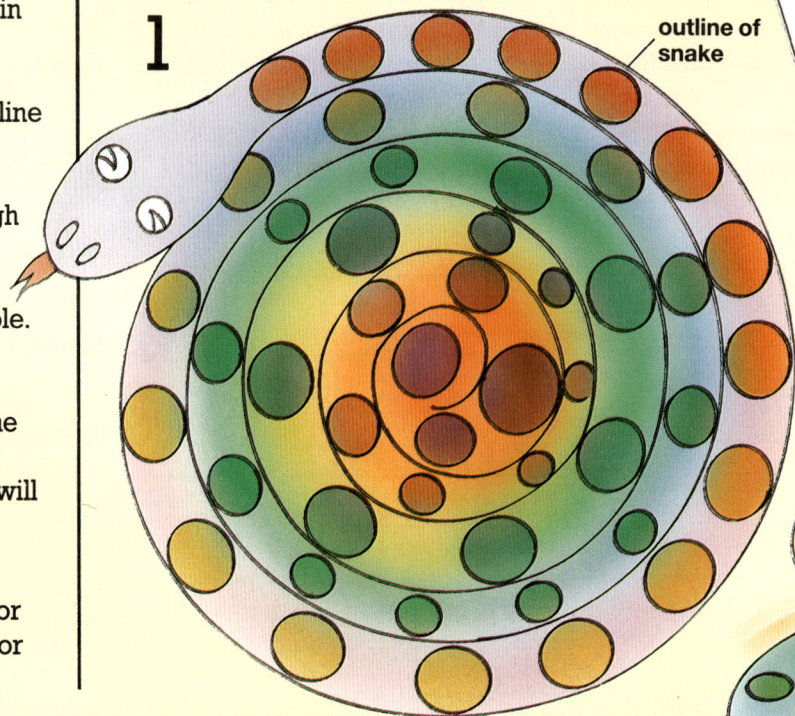

1

outline of snake

thin card or paper

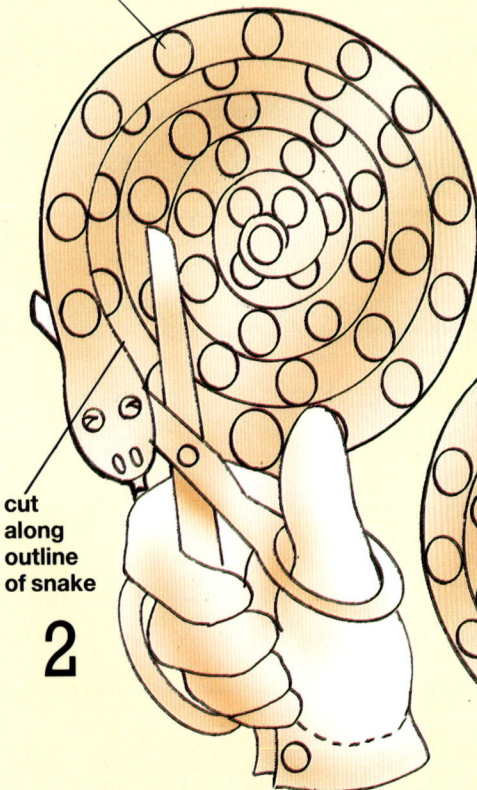

cut along outline of snake

2

thread cotton through hole in snake's tail

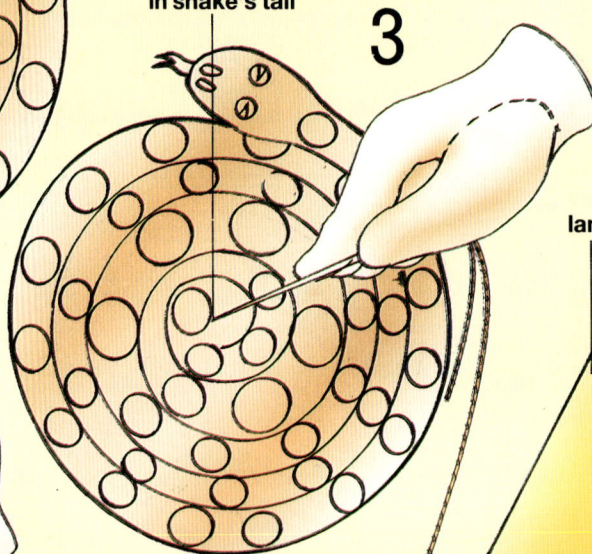

3

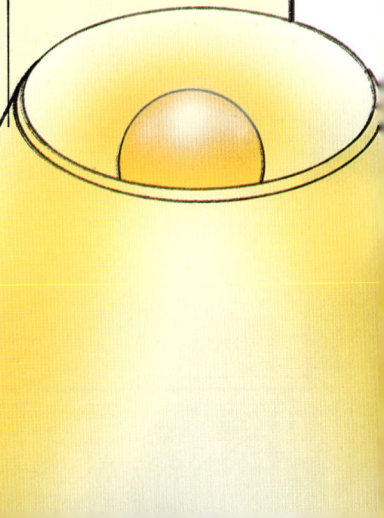

4

heat current causes snake to revolve

lamp

CHRISTMAS TREE FAIRY

Cut a snake as before but this time use aluminium kitchen foil.

1 Trace the shape shown below to make the fairy. Cut this from kitchen foil too but make it double thickness for strength.

2 Leave an extended piece that can be bent back to make a base.

3 Use a popper as a bearing. Stick the popper to the base of the fairy with a touch of adhesive.

4 Stick the foil snake to the popper by its head. Use a needle pushed into the end of a balsa wood rod as a pivot for the fairy.

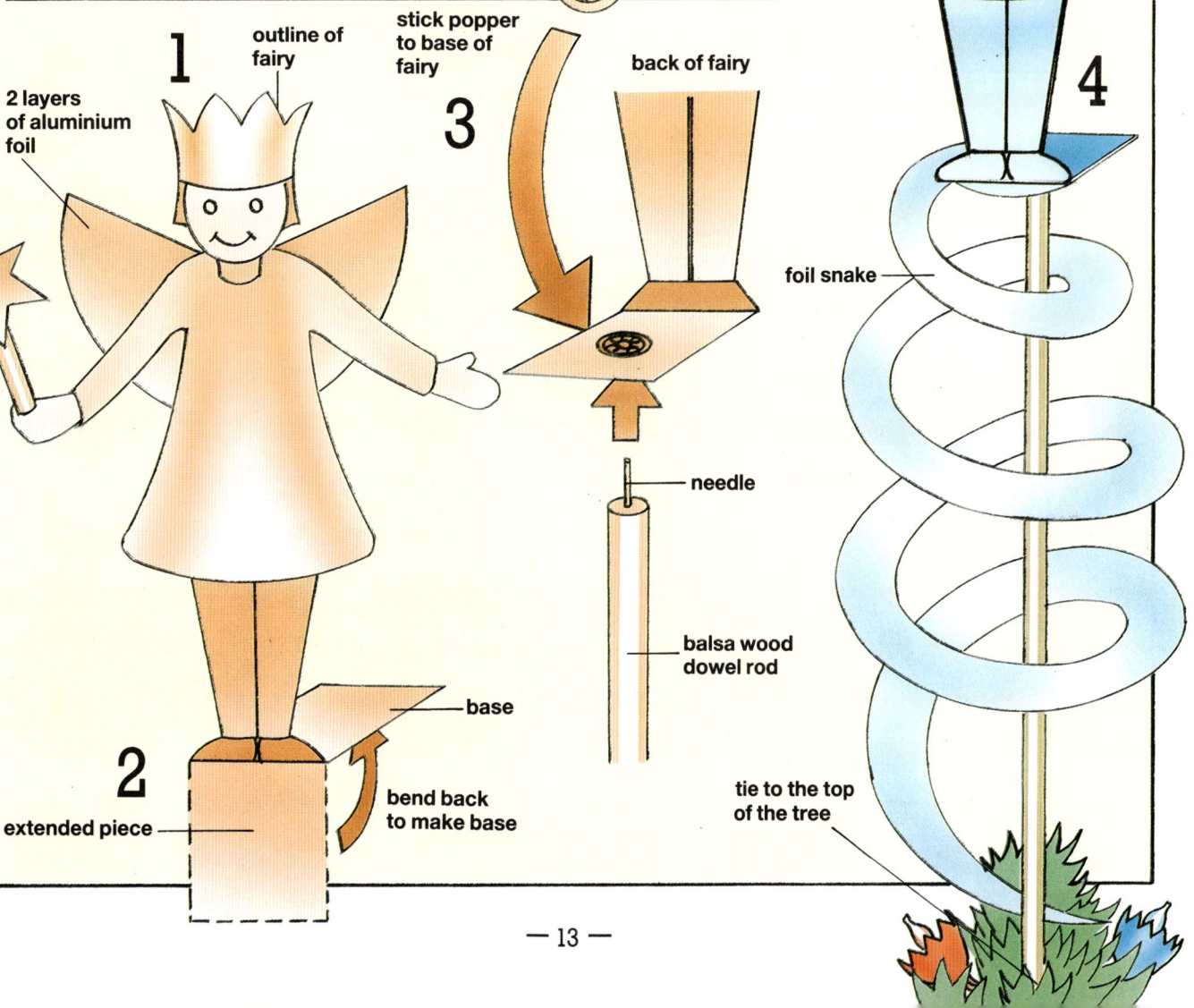

The fairy will revolve well on the Christmas Tree if a clutch of fairy lights are put just beneath it.

1 outline of fairy

2 layers of aluminium foil

3 stick popper to base of fairy

back of fairy

2 extended piece

base

bend back to make base

needle

balsa wood dowel rod

4 foil snake

tie to the top of the tree

MAGIC SQUARES

Magic squares were invented many centuries ago by the Chinese. The earliest form is shown on the right, the 'lo-shu' as it is called. Can you see what is magic about it? Count the dots in each row, column and both diagonals.

1 Whether you add up, down or across the answer always comes to 15. Three times the central number.

This square is so magical that people still wear it as a lucky charm. This is an order 3 magic square since it has 3 rows and 3 columns. You can make lots of order 3 squares to try on your friends.

2 Add 3 to every number in the original square.

The answers to the additions are 24. That is to say three times the central number.

Try adding other numbers.

3 Multiply every number in the original square by 4.

The answer to the additions is 60. Three times the central number.

Try multiplying by other numbers.

the earliest form of magic square is called the 'lo-shu'

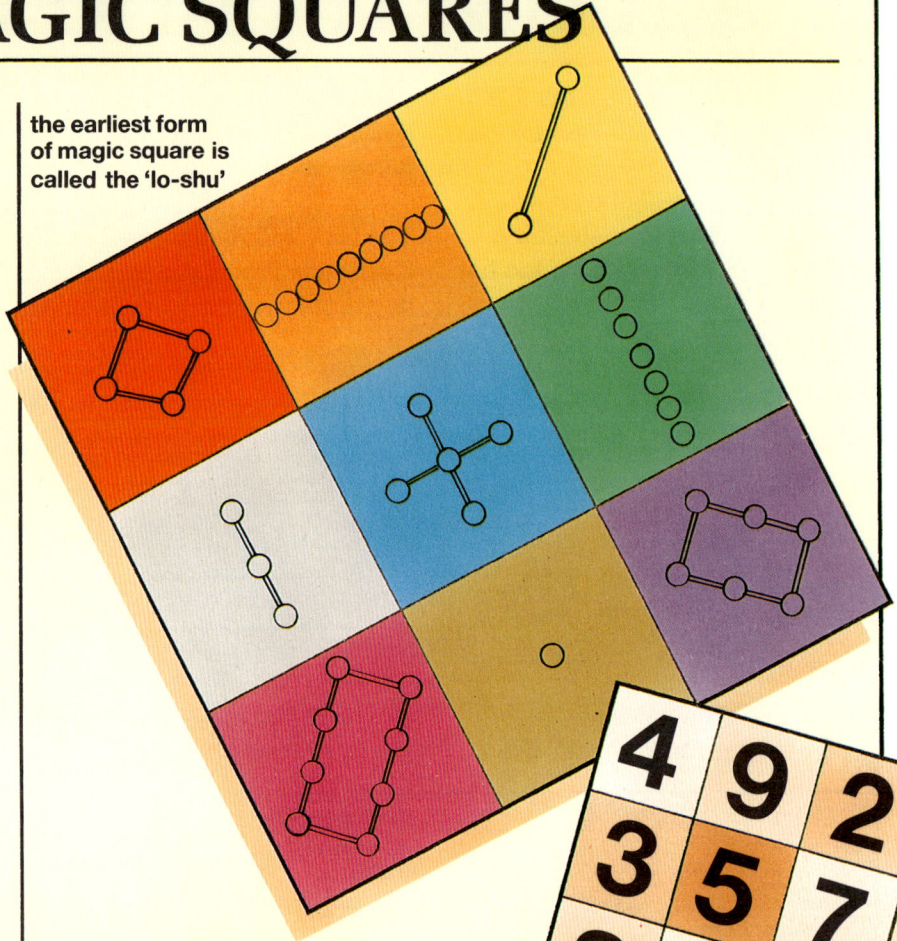

1

4	9	2
3	5	7
8	1	6

an order 3 magic square

2

7	12	5
6	8	10
11	4	9

Add 3 to every number in the original square.

3

16	36	8
12	20	28
32	4	24

Multiply every number in the original square by 4.

an order
4 magic square

4 by 4 grid

To make an order 4 magic square enter the numbers 1 to 16 (or any other 16 consecutive numbers) onto a 4 by 4 grid as shown left.

1 Change the corner numbers on the diagonals.

2 Changeover the four centre numbers on the diagonals.

3 Fill in the remaining numbers in the same positions as at the beginning.

If you add all rows, columns or diagonals they come to 34. You also get 34 if you add the four central numbers.

1
Change the corner numbers on the diagonals.

2
Changeover the 4 centre numbers on the diagonals.

3
Fill in the remaining numbers in the same positions as at the beginning.

TANGRAMS

Another Chinese invention is the tangram. It is a seven piece puzzle.

1 It is easily constructed if you use the sixteen square grid shown to help you draw the seven pieces. These then need to be cut out. You could colour them in if you like.

2 Can you remake the square from the seven pieces?

3 The Chinese use the pieces to make all sorts of figures like the examples below. You try.

square

16 square grid

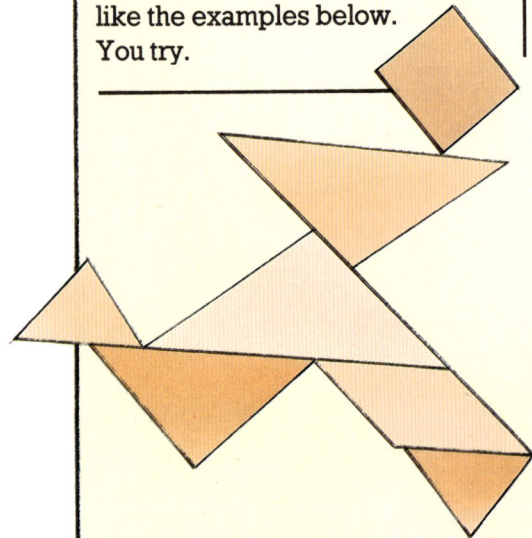

cut out the 7 pieces from card

more tangrams to make

MAGIC EGGS

1 Trace the template of the magic egg onto card.

2 Cut out the seven pieces and colour them in.

3 What birds can you hatch using your seven pieces?

template of egg for tracing

colour in pieces

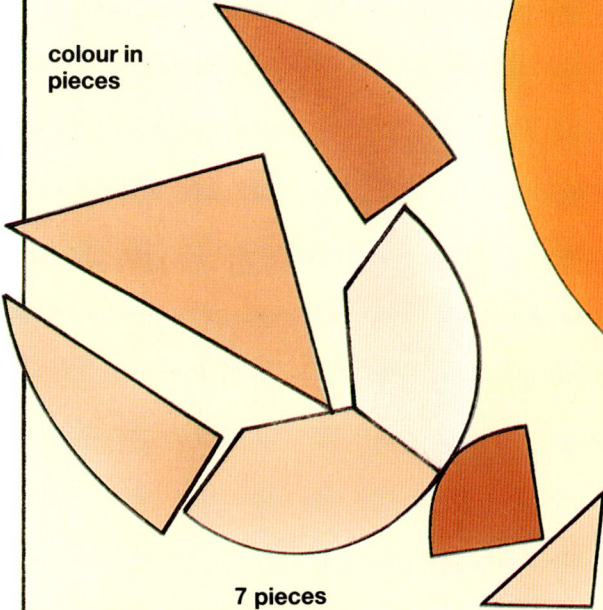

7 pieces

Can you make any other birds with your 7 pieces?

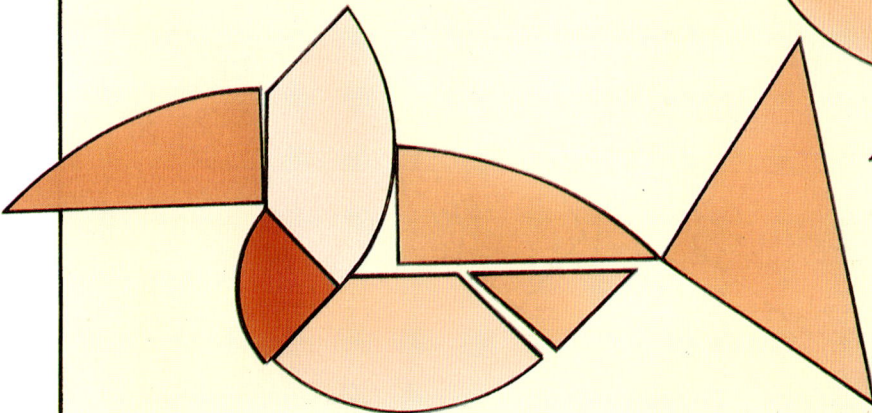

3-D DESK CALENDAR

1 Trace this 5 sided shape called a pentagon onto card. Cut it out to make a template.

2 Draw round the template to construct the two nets shown below on thick paper or thin card. Remember to draw the flaps too.

3 Cut out the nets. Fold all the flaps and score along all the sides of the inner pentagon.

4 Glue the two nets together to make a 12 sided shape called a dodecahedron.

5 Each face of the dodecahedron will hold the calendar for one month of the year. Write one month on each face. You may find it easier to write up your calendar before you join your two nets together.

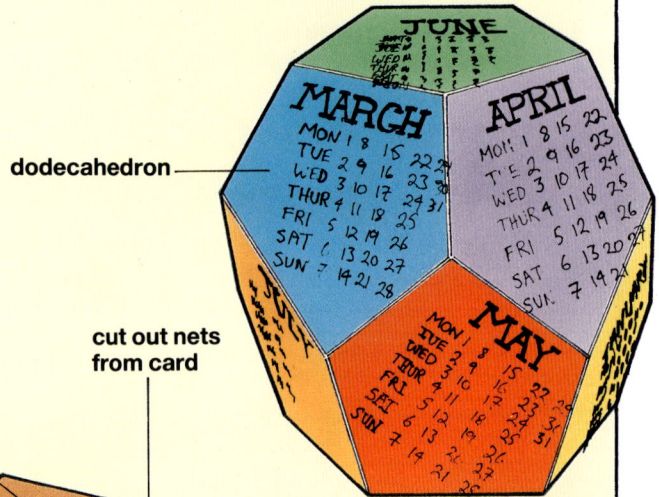

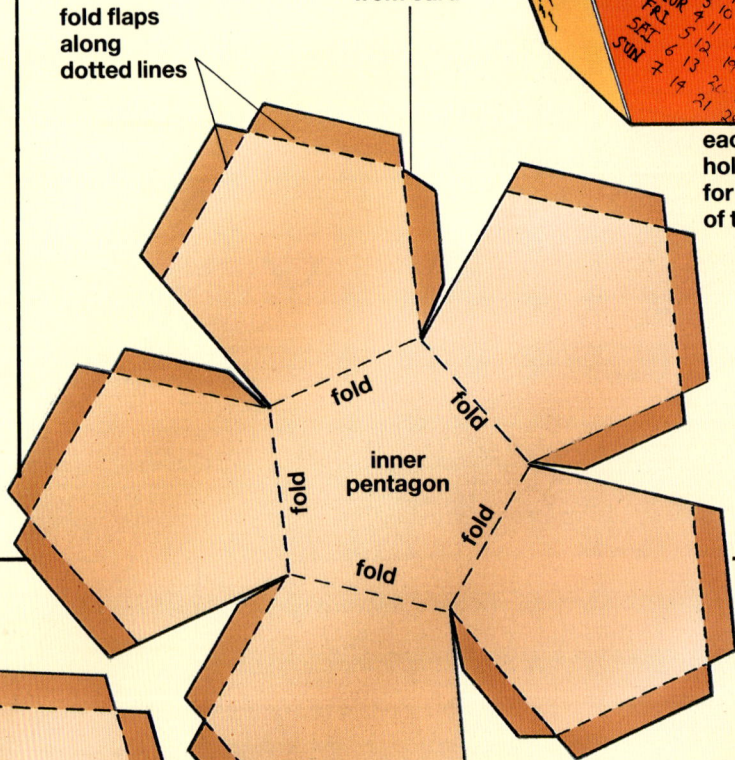

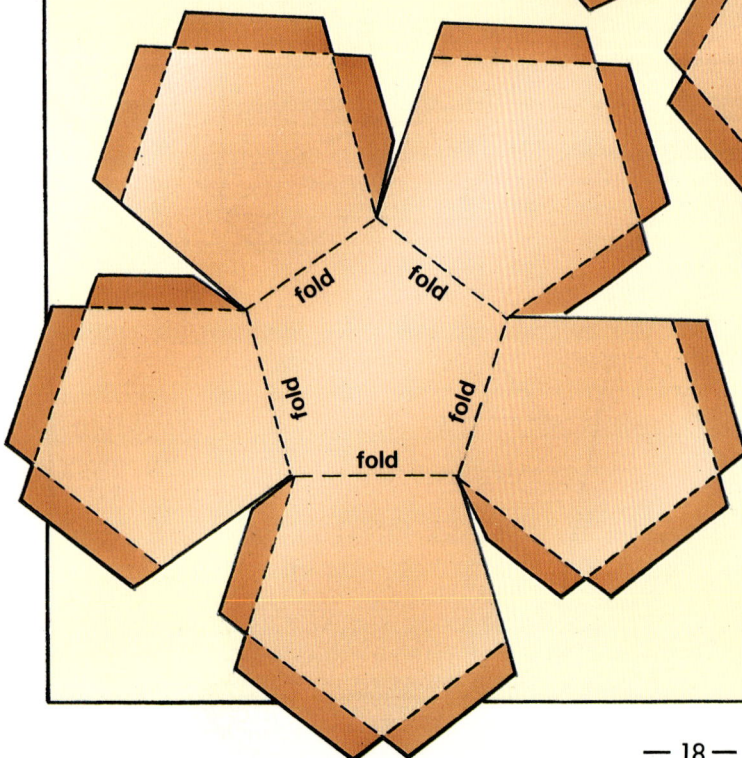

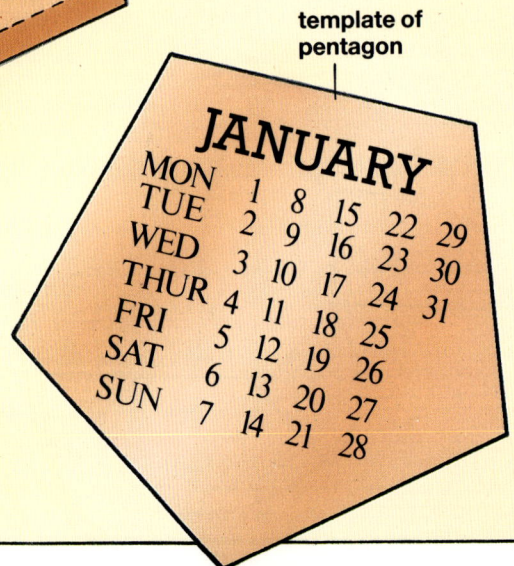

dodecahedron

each face holds calendar for one month of the year

cut out nets from card

fold flaps along dotted lines

fold

fold

fold

fold

fold

inner pentagon

fold

fold

fold

fold

fold

fold

template of pentagon

JANUARY

MON	1	8	15	22	29
TUE	2	9	16	23	30
WED	3	10	17	24	31
THUR	4	11	18	25	
FRI	5	12	19	26	
SAT	6	13	20	27	
SUN	7	14	21	28	

OTHER 3-D SHAPES

The dodecahedron is a regular solid. There are four other regular solids: the cube, tetrahedron, octahedron and icosahedron. The nets for each of these solids are shown below.

1 Trace each net onto thin card. Cut it out. Score along all the dotted lines.

2 Shape and glue each solid. When they are made you can hang them by cotton from a shelf. You can hang a dodecahedron too.

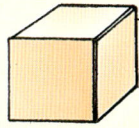
cube

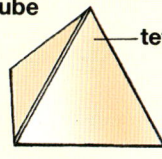
tetrahedron

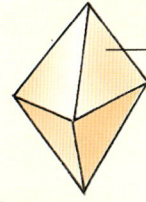
octahedron

icosahedron

hang shapes by cotton from a shelf

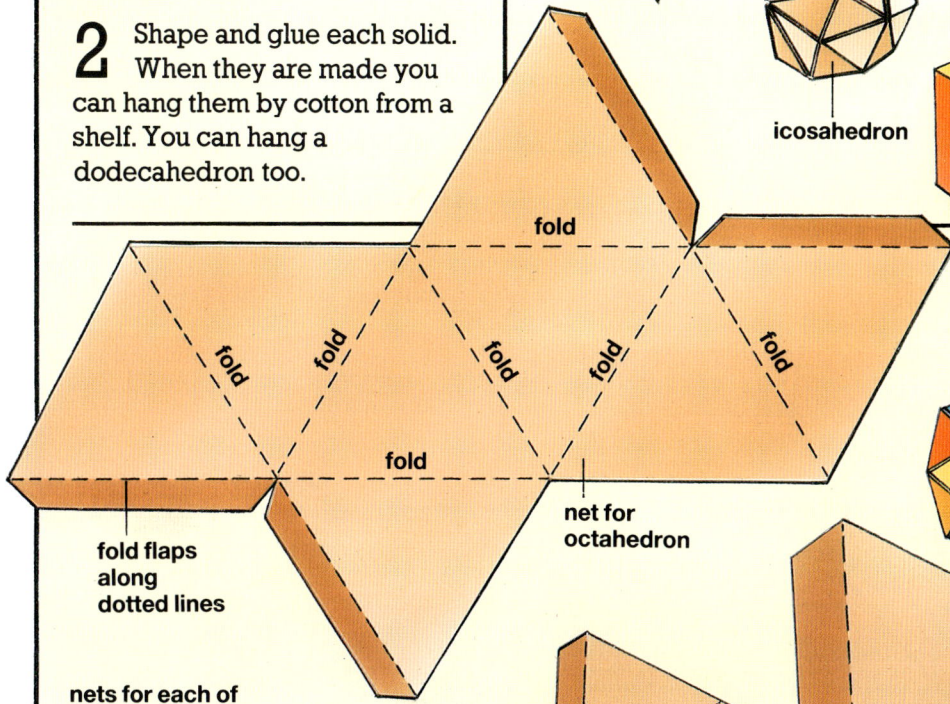

fold flaps along dotted lines

net for octahedron

nets for each of the solids

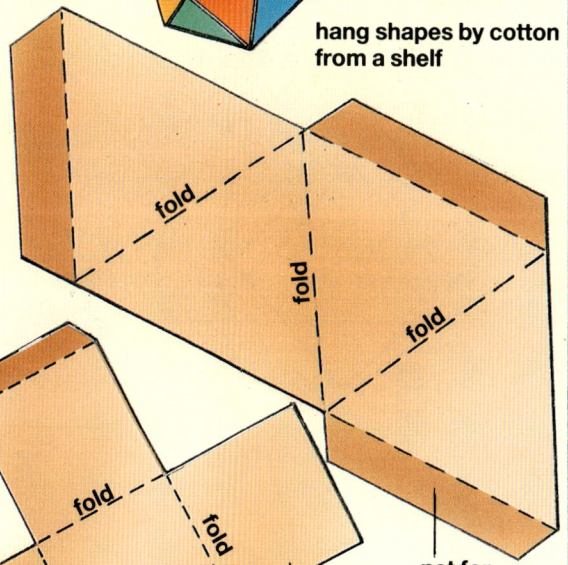

net for tetrahedron

net for cube

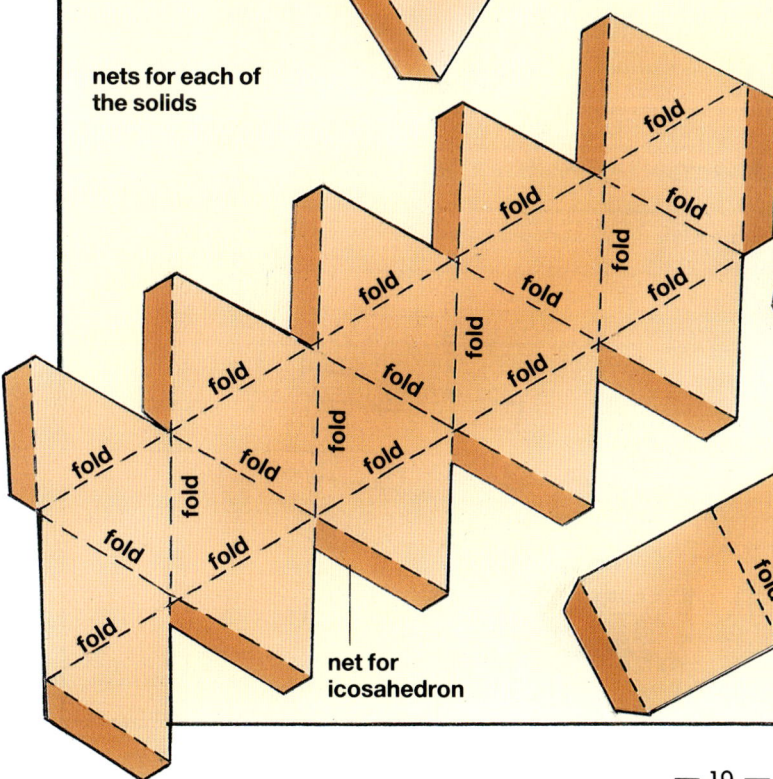

net for icosahedron

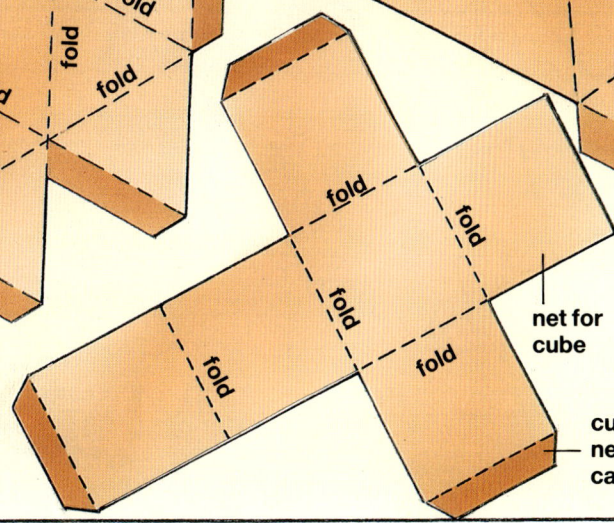

cut out nets from card

CHRISTMAS CARD

1 Trace and cut out these four templates A, B, C, D from card.

2 Cut out the two slits in template D as shown.

3 Colour in Santa Claus, template A.

4 Thread the long narrow strip C through the two slits in the large card D. Stick Santa Claus to strip C. Lightly glue the fireplace B to each side of the card. Let it dry.

5 Pull on the strip to make Santa Claus appear. Push on the strip to send him back up the chimney. Decorate the chimney breast.

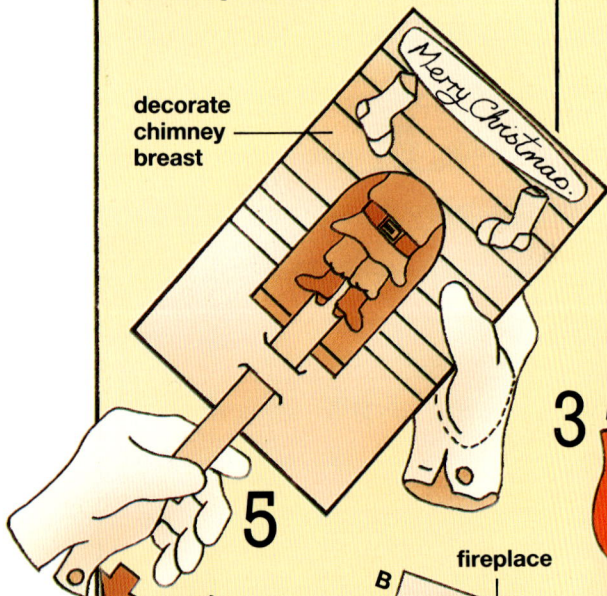

templates for tracing

1

B

C

D

decorate chimney breast

Merry Christmas.

5

fireplace

3 A

B

D

chimney

slits

2

glue

glue

4

A

C

GET WELL CARD

1 Trace and cut these templates A B C below from card. Cut out the shaded portions on the large card A.

2 Draw the mouse on the narrow strip of card C.

3 Fix the small card oblong B at the back of the large card A with a touch of glue at the top and at the bottom.

Assemble.

4 Push and pull the strip to make the mouse appear and disappear.

Decorate the card.

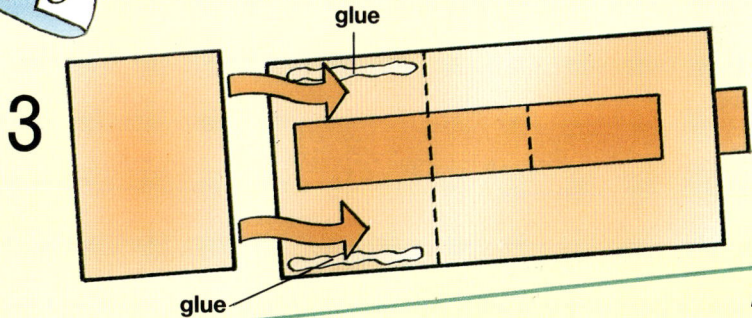

GET WELL SOON

4

glue

3

glue

templates for tracing

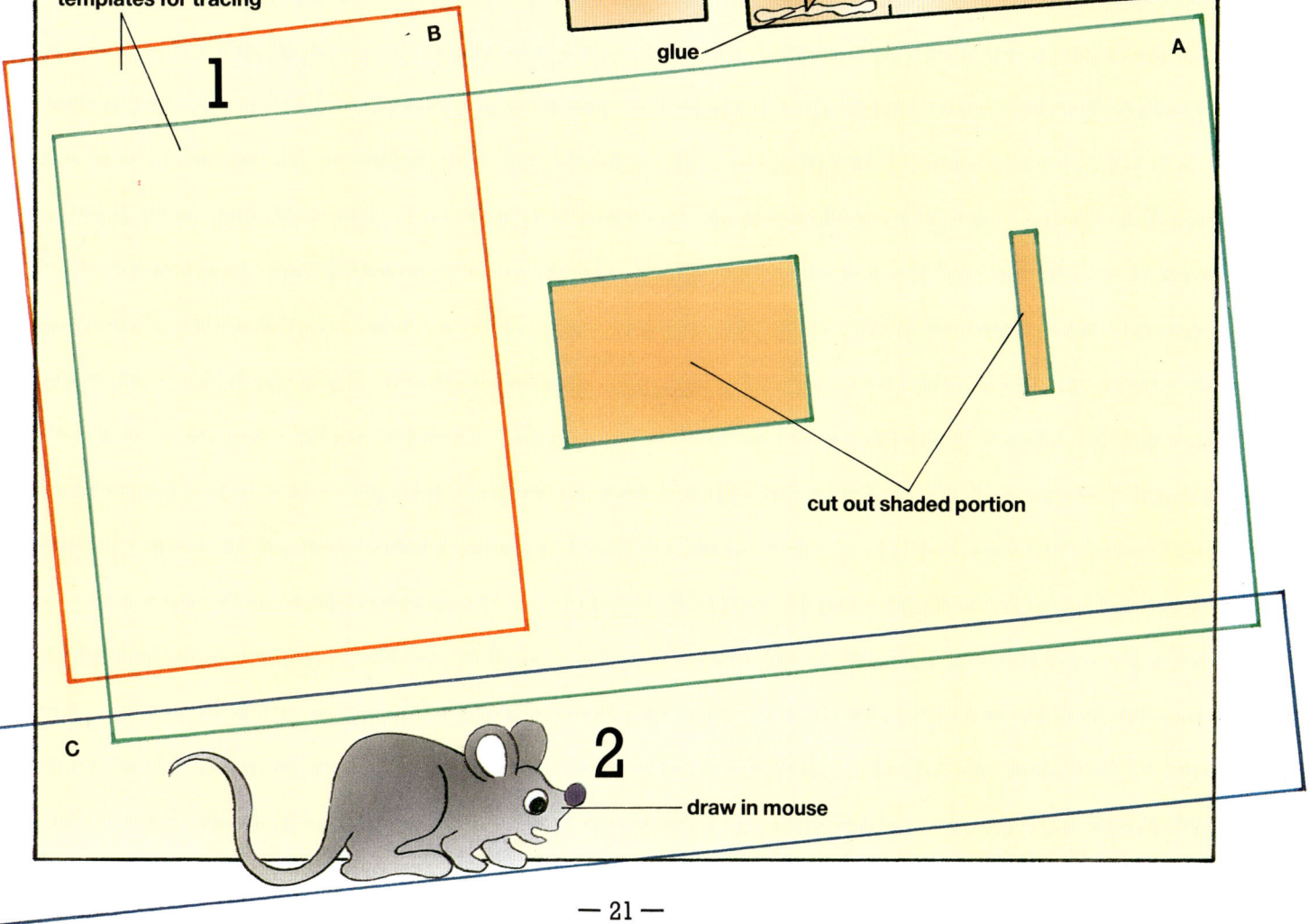

B

1

A

cut out shaded portion

C

2

draw in mouse

NEW YEAR CARD

1 Trace the three templates A B C onto card. Cut them out. Cut slits in template A, one long slit and one curved slit, as shown below.

2 Fix the T-shaped template B to the main card A with a paper fastener. The long arm of the T should protrude through the long slit, and the short arm should stick through the curved slit.

3 Stick the bell to the short protruding arm. Moving the long arm will make the bell move.

4 Decorate the card and ring in the New Year.

4

RING IN THE NEW YEAR

C

2

long arm of T protrudes

paper fastener

glue

3

templates for tracing

1

cut a long straight slit

B

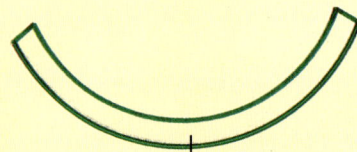

cut a curved slit

A

MOBILES

Balancing structures like this are called mobiles. Try making one from string and thin plant canes. You can tie on all sorts of things. Always begin balancing from the bottom up.

1 Take one cane. Tie a piece of string at its centre. Balance the cane from this string and objects either side of the string, carefully adjusting them so that you get a balance.

2 Do the same thing with a separate piece of cane. Now tie these two canes to a cane dangling above them.

odds and ends mobile

thin plant cane

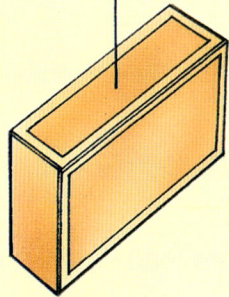

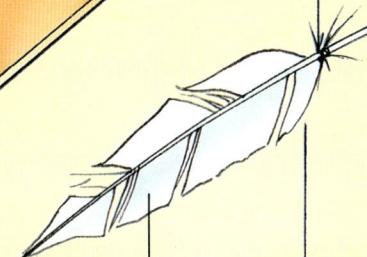

shapes mobile

tie string at centre of cane

attach canes to cane above, always working from the bottom up

tie on all sorts of objects

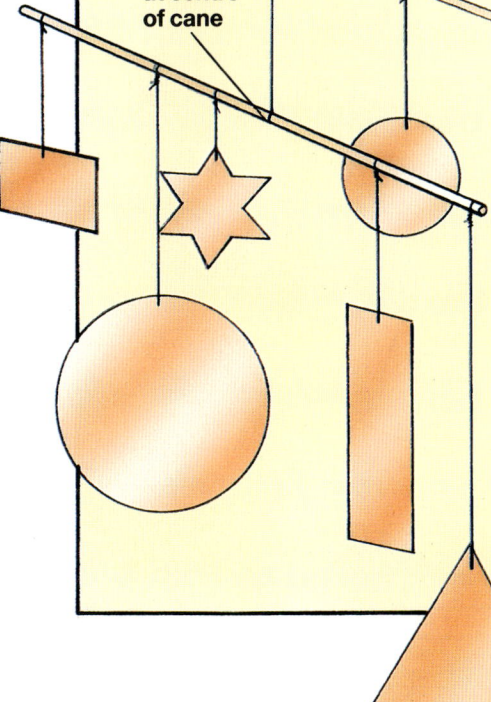

pop stars mobile

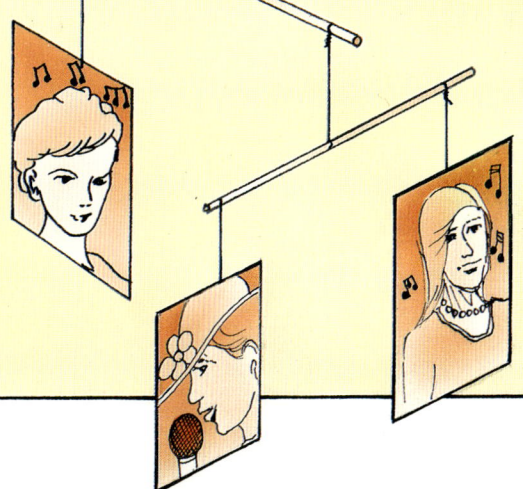

TWO-WAY PICTURE

1 Choose two coloured magazine pictures. Either make sure they are both exactly the same size, or cut them to the same size.

2 Take a piece of thin card the same height as the magazine cuttings. Fold it into concertina pleats 10 millimetres wide. Cut picture one into 10 millimetre strips.

3 Glue these 10 millimetre strips each in turn onto the left-facing pleats. Cut the second picture into 10 millimetre strips and again glue these in turn onto the right-facing pleats.

If you look at your concertina folder from the left you will see one picture. If you view from the right you will see the other.

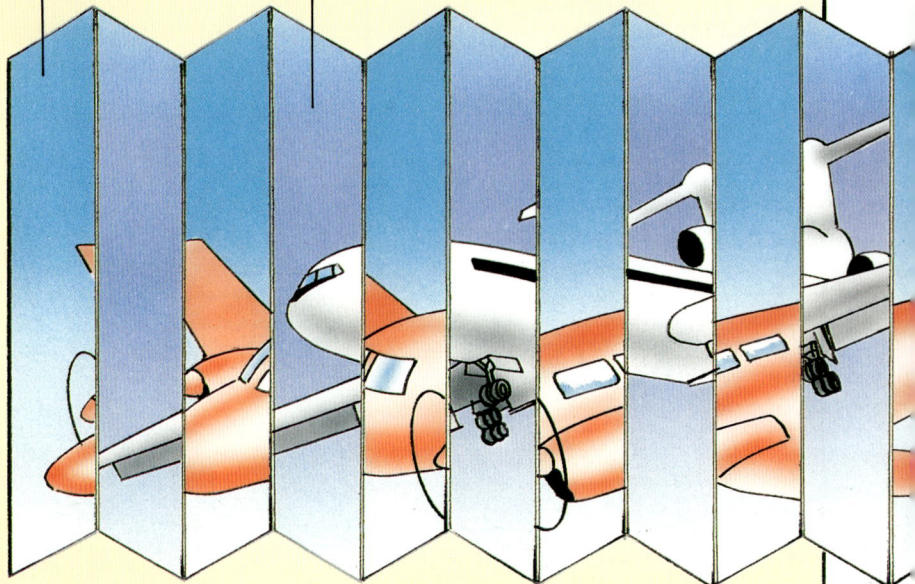

glue strips from picture 1 to left-facing pleats

glue strips from picture 2 to right-facing pleats

concertina folder

3

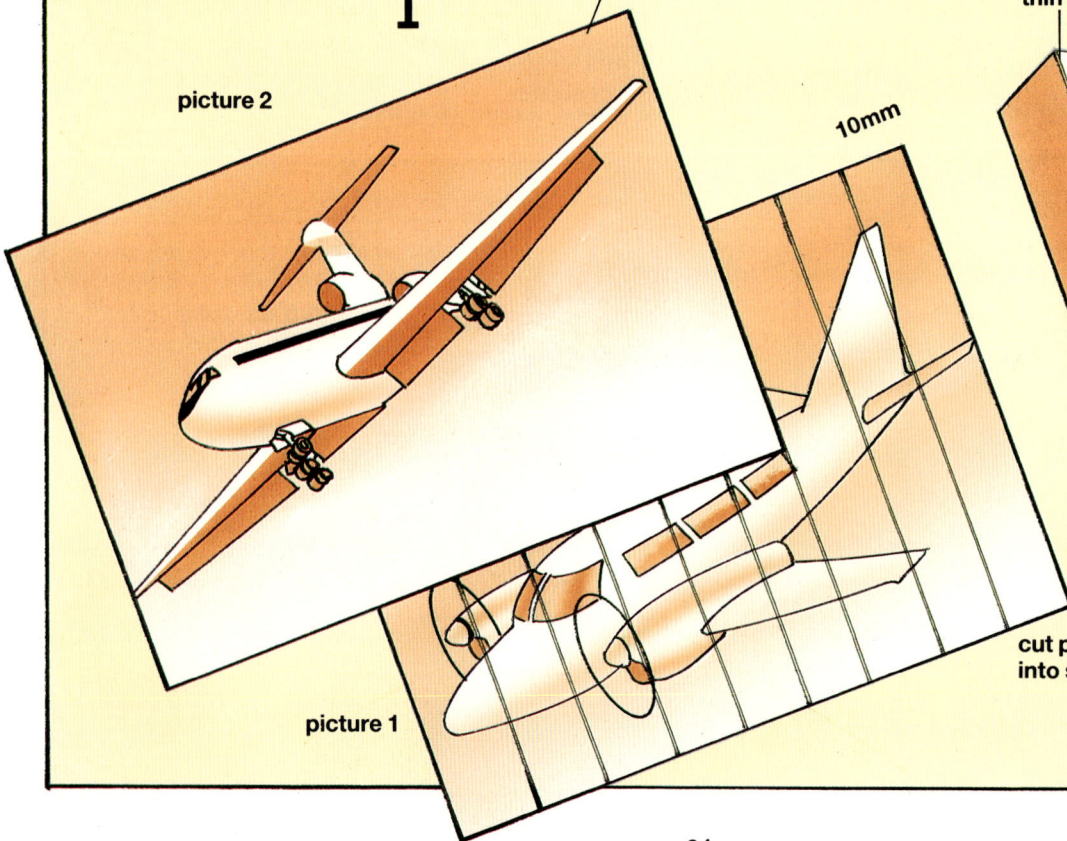

magazine pictures

thin card

1

picture 2

10mm

picture 1

10mm

2 fold into concertina pleats

cut pictures into strips

THREE-WAY PICTURE

1 For this, three magazine pictures are needed. Again they must all be the same size. Number your pictures 1–3.

2 Cut a piece of card to the same height and the total length of the three pictures. Crease the card into 10 millimetre lengths. Number it 1, 2, 3; 1, 2, 3. . . as shown.

3 Bend the card so that it makes the pattern of the folds (X), show.

4 Cut each magazine picture into 10 millimetre strips. Glue strips from your picture 1 to the card wherever the number 1 is shown. You will see that this means gluing the first strip at the edge, missing two strips of card, then gluing the next picture strip in position. Continue gluing one and missing two until you finish picture.

Glue strips from your pictures 2 and 3 in the same way in the positions shown.

5 Fold the concertina so that every third strip remains flat.

View the concertina folder from the left to see one picture, from the front to see another, and from the right to see yet another.

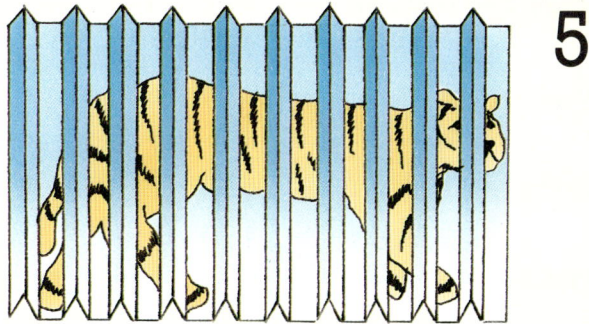

5

front

left

right

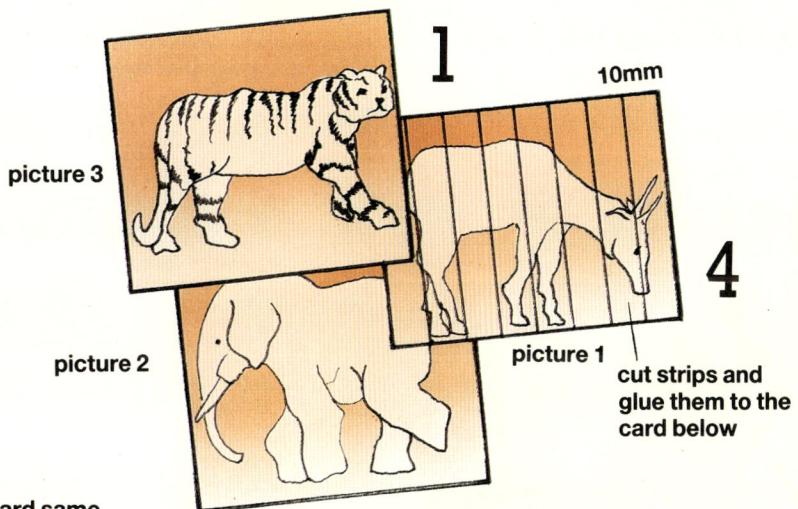

1

10mm

picture 3

picture 2

picture 1

4

cut strips and glue them to the card below

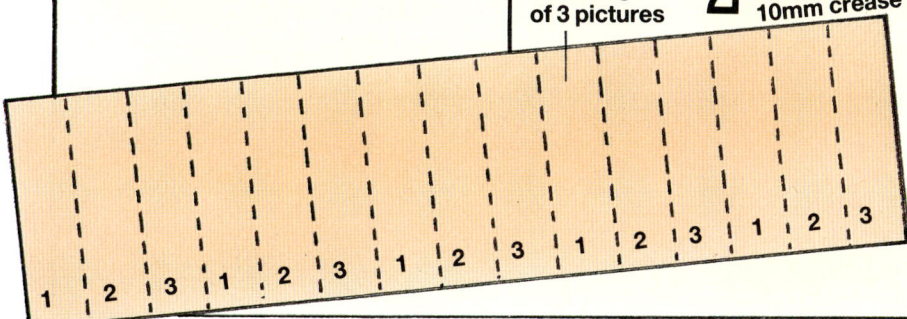

card same height and total length of 3 pictures

2 10mm crease

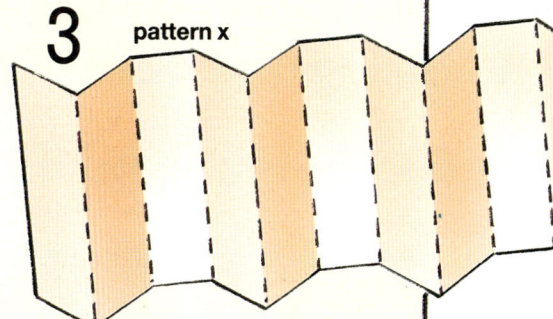

3 pattern x

bend card

POP UP CARDS

Greeting cards that pop up when you open them are very popular.

They are easy to make.

1 Trace the balloon and butterfly onto thin card. Colour them in and cut them out.

2 Trace two copies of the V shape and cut these from card too. Score each V shape along the dotted lines.

3 Take a sheet of thin card and fold it to make your greetings card. Fold and glue your V shape into this folded card as shown.

4 Glue the long 'tail' of the butterfly as illustrated.

5 Attach the balloon by a piece of cotton and glue.

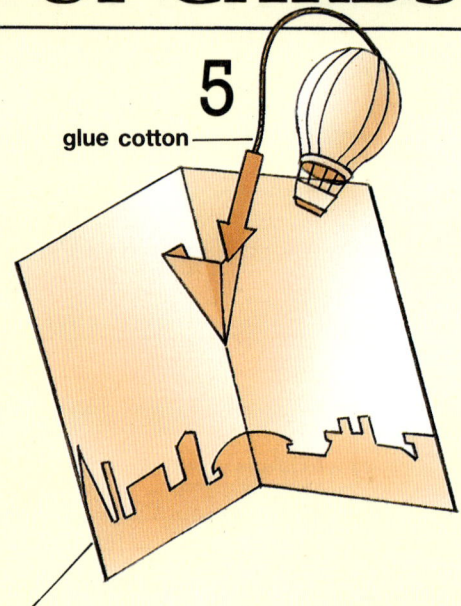

5

glue cotton

thin card

balloon outline

1

butterfly outline

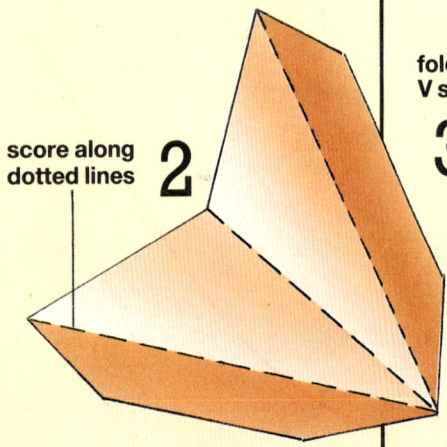

2 score along dotted lines

3 fold and glue V shape into card

folded card

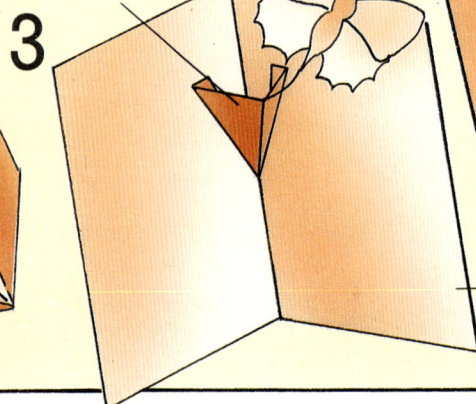

4 glue long tail

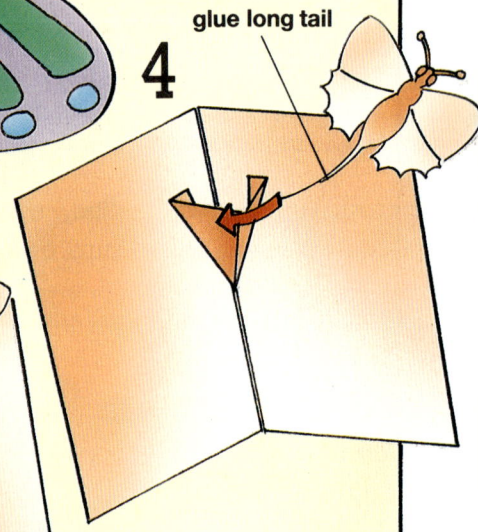

PICTURE PATTERNS

There was a famous Dutch artist, called M.C. Escher who was fascinated with the way images fitted together. Here are some examples of the sort of pictures he painted. You can see how the images interlink, one with another to cover the whole surface without any overlap or gap. On the next page there are images of birds and ghosts for you to trace and use to make interlinking patterns.

the shapes interlink without any overlap or gaps

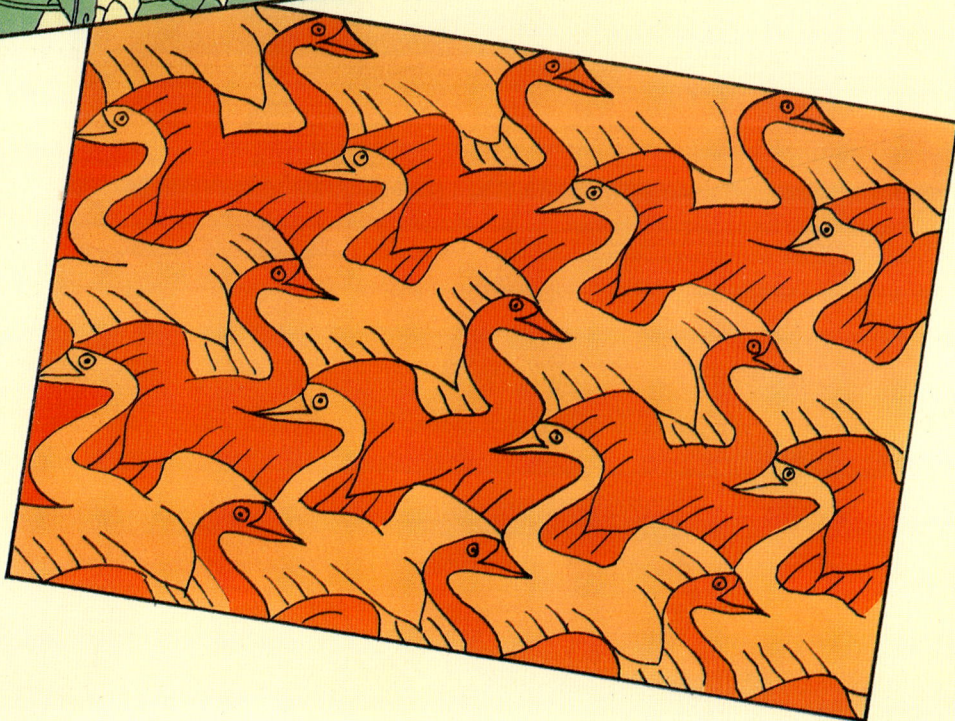

BIRDS

1 Trace a number of these birds onto thin card.

2 Colour them in bright colours and cut them out and fit them into an interlinking pattern as M.C. Escher did in his paintings.

templates of birds for tracing

cut out shapes from thin card

fit birds into an interlinking pattern

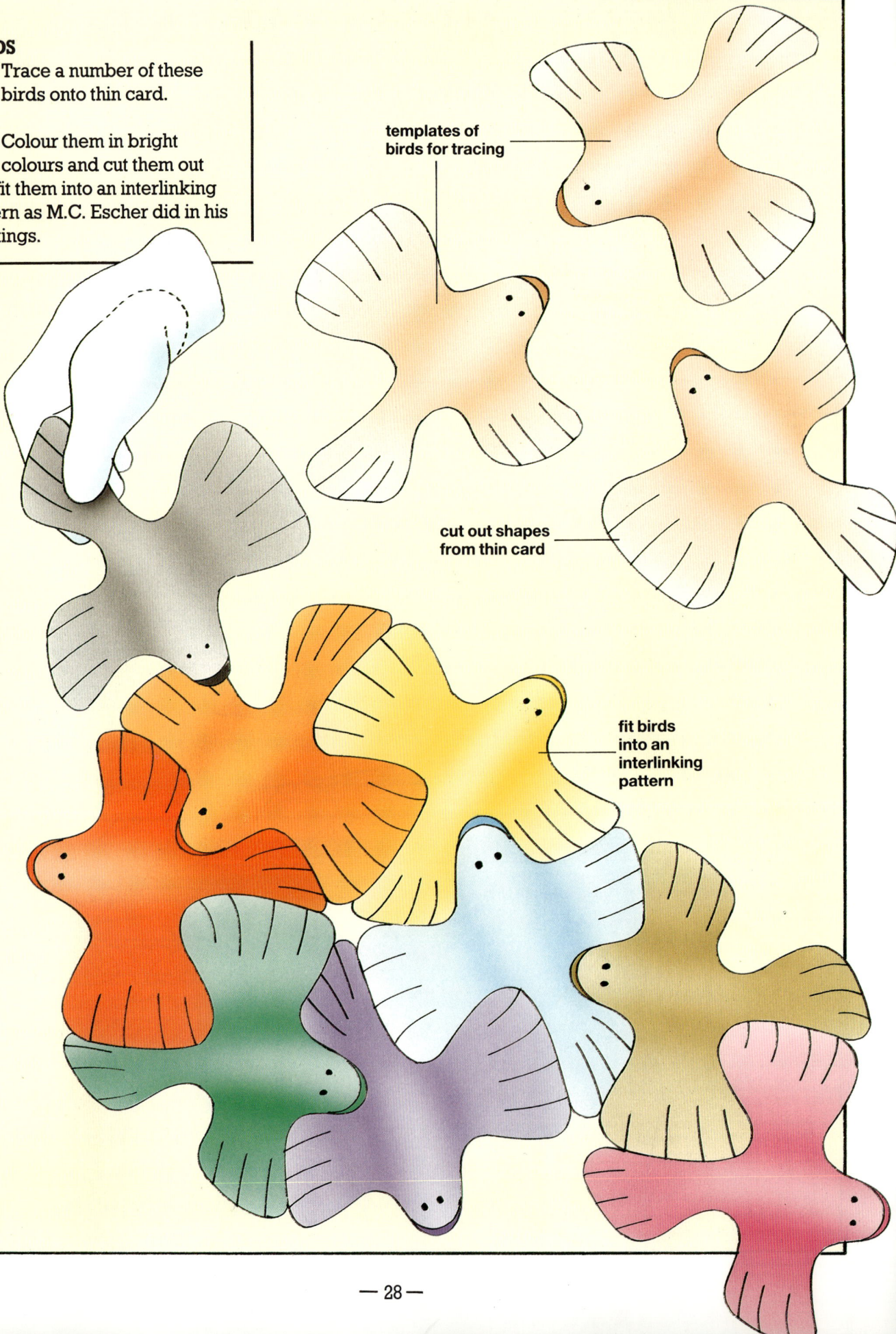

GHOSTS
Try doing the same with ghost shapes or you could use one ghost as a template and draw round it to make an interlinking pattern.

template of ghostly birds for tracing

fit cut out shapes of ghostly birds into an interlinking pattern

fit cut out shapes into an interlinking pattern

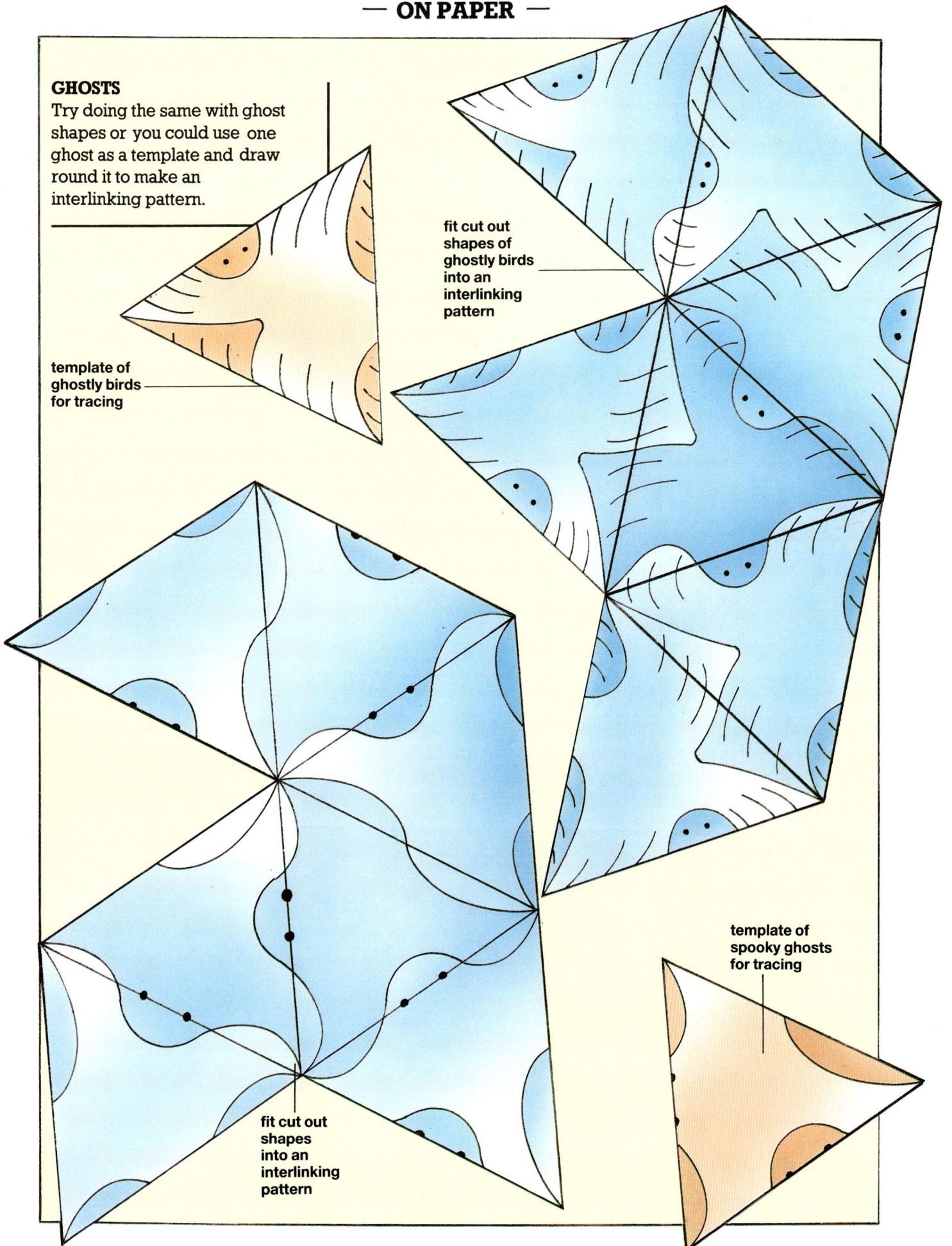

template of spooky ghosts for tracing

CYCLOPS, A ONE-EYED MONSTER

More shapes to trace, cut out and tesselate or fit together into patterns.

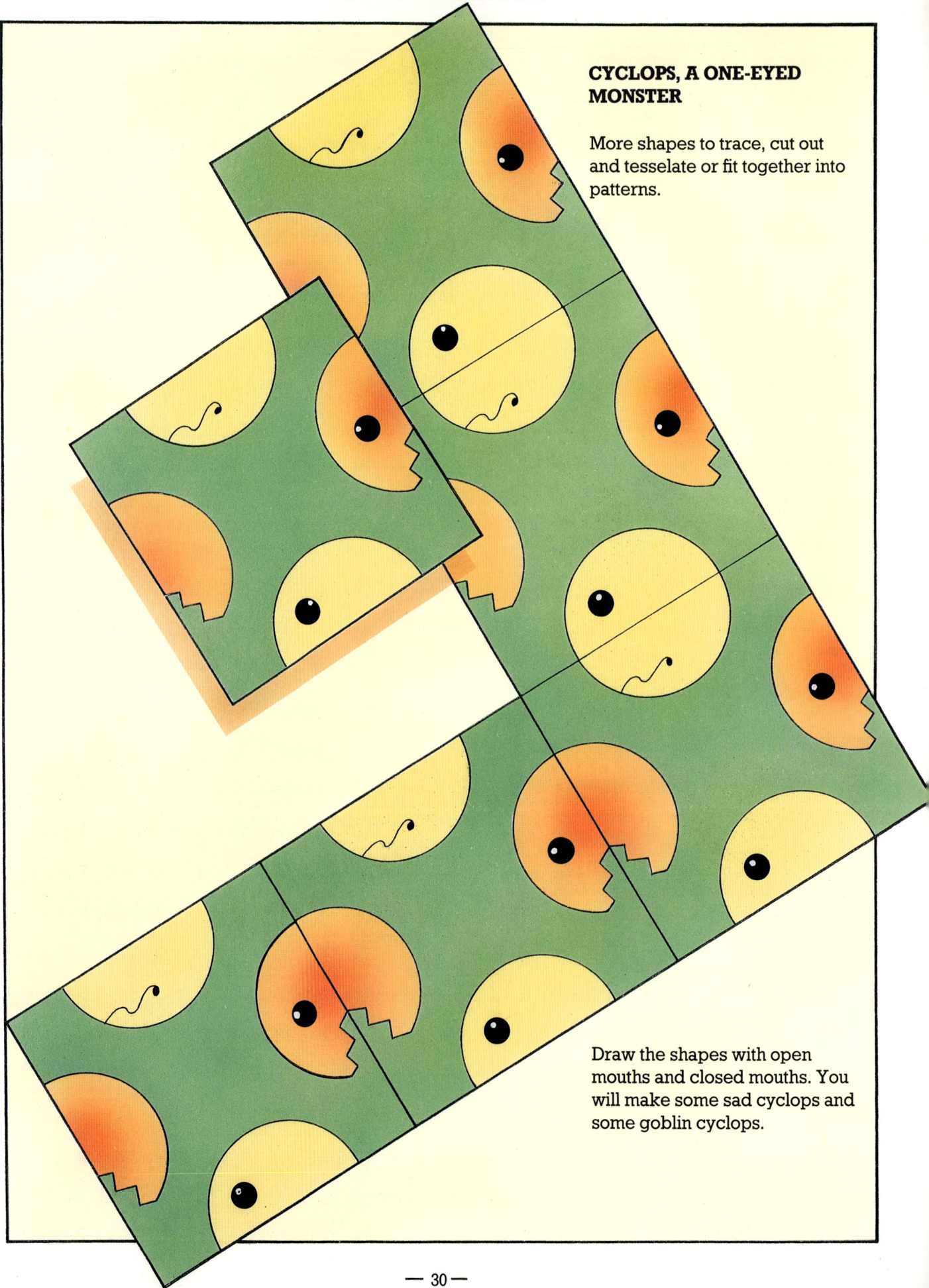

Draw the shapes with open mouths and closed mouths. You will make some sad cyclops and some goblin cyclops.

PLUMBER'S NIGHTMARE

You can make more complex
designs as this pattern shows.

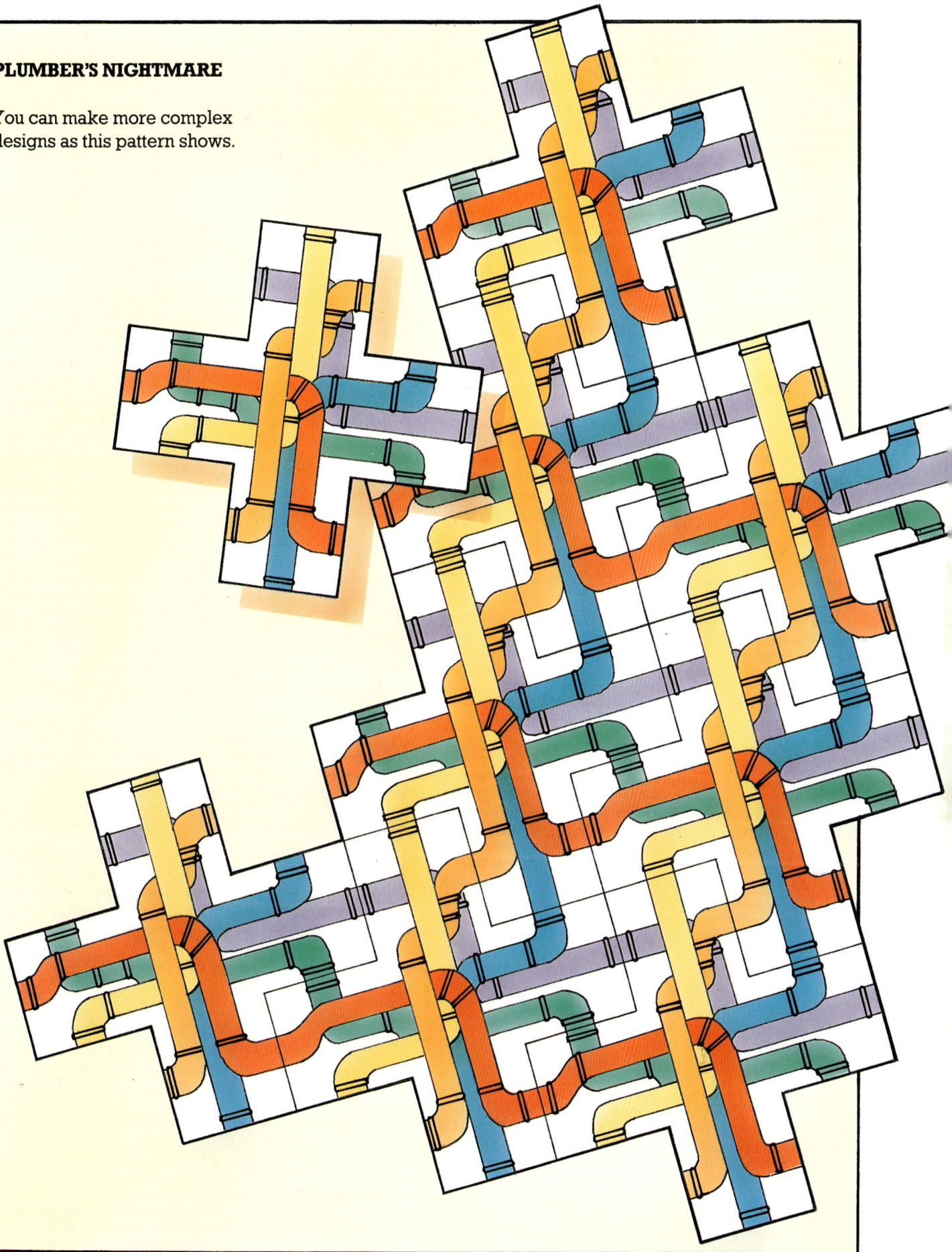

NOTES FOR PARENTS AND TEACHERS

Pages 3 – 7 Things fall because of a force of attraction towards the centre of the earth. We are constantly adjusting our centre of gravity, albeit subconsciously, as we move. However, we originally as very small children had to learn how to do this. These pages are concerned with centre of gravity games and toys, being concerned with how to get a balance about a central point.

Pages 8 – 9 Children are learning that sounds are produced by vibrating objects. You do not get a sound without making something vibrate.

Page 8 The bull roarer vibrates when spun making its peculiar noise.

Page 9 The buzzsaw causes a vibration of the paper making a high pitched sound.

Pages 10 – 11 These pages describe two clocks. In one we tell the time by the sun, in the other by the stars. Children's attention will be drawn to the apparent daily motion of both sun and stars. They will realise that the day length changes throughout the year and be able to measure time using their clocks.

Page 10 The sundial shown is a typical sundial. The raised central portion is called the gnomon. The angle of the gnomon to the horizontal varies with the latitude of where you live. For example in London it is 51.5°, while in New York it is 41°.

The graduations on the sundial are not an equal distance apart.

This table gives their position.

Sundial Time	Angle for London (Latitude 51.5°)
6 am	0
7	19
8	36.5
9	52
10	65.5
11	78
12	90
1 pm	102
2	114.5
3	128
4	143.5
5	161
6	180

You draw the 4 am and 5 am marks diametrically opposite the 4 pm and 5 pm marks; with the 7 pm and 8 pm marks diametrically opposite the 7 am and 8 am ones.

This information is correct for London. In other countries you would need to look up your latitude in an atlas. Make your gnomon to the angle of that latitude. Choose a sunny day! Set up your sundial and plot the angles of the shadows cast on the hour through the day. You could then measure the angles formed and make a table like the one shown for London.

Page 11 This clock will, of course, rotate anticlockwise since the stars appear to spin in an anti-clockwise manner. In the southern hemisphere you need to choose appropriate constellations.

Pages 12 – 13 Both these models illustrate how warm air rises, that is they work on convection currents.

Pages 14 – 15 Magic squares show how numbers can intrigue and at the same time illustrate how they do not behave in a wayward manner but give pattern. Looking for pattern is at the heart of mathematics.

Pages 16 – 17 Tangrams give children scope for inventing all sorts of patterns and figures, and at the same time help develop the concept of area as amount of surface covered.

Pages 18 – 19 The 3D structures described on these pages are the Platonic solids. They are the only regular solids. They were invented by Plato, and the Greeks used them as symbols: tetrahedron (fire), octahedron (air), cube (earth), icosahedron (water), dodecahedron (universe).

Pages 20 – 23 The cards and the mobiles all use levers as their working principle. That is to say they all use a bar turning about a point.

Pages 24 – 25 Two and three way pictures like these greatly intrigued our Victorian ancestors. Making them draws attention to how our position in relation to objects affects how we see them. Changing our position in relation to the models made on these two pages completely changes the picture we see.

Page 26 Pop up cards take children into paper engineering.

Pages 27 – 31 Tesselating shapes and picture patterns not only introduce children to the fitting of shapes together but are an early and very important introduction to the concept of area as amount of surface covered.